YOUTH SUICIDE

YOUTH SUICIDE

Issues, Assessment, and Intervention

Edited by

PETER CIMBOLIC, PH.D.
The Catholic University of America

DAVID A. JOBES, PH.D.
The Catholic University of America

CHARLES C THOMAS • PUBLISHER
Springfield • Illinois • U.S.A.

Published and Distributed Throughout the World by

CHARLES C THOMAS • PUBLISHER
2600 South First Street
Springfield, Illinois 62794-9265

© *1990 by* CHARLES C THOMAS • PUBLISHER

ISBN 0-398-05706-0

Library of Congress Catalog Card Number: 90-11090

With THOMAS BOOKS *careful attention is given to all details of manufacturing
and design. It is the Publisher's desire to present books that are satisfactory as to their
physical qualities and artistic possibilities and appropriate for their particular use.*
THOMAS BOOKS *will be true to those laws of quality that assure a good name
and good will.*

Printed in the United States of America
SC-R-3

Library of Congress Cataloging-in-Publication Data

Youth Suicide : issues, assessment, and intervention / edited by Peter
  Cimbolic, David A. Jobes.
    p. cm.
  Includes bibliographical references.
  Includes index.
  ISBN 0-398-05706-0
  1. Youth—United States—Suicidal behavior. 2. Suicide—United
States—Prevention. I. Cimbolic, Peter. II. Jobes, David A.
  [DNLM: 1. Suicide—in adolescence. 2. Suicide—prevention &
control. HV 6546 Y834]
HV6546.Y683 1990
362.2'8'0835—dc20
DNLM/DLC
for Library of Congress   90-11090
                                 CIP

CONTRIBUTORS

Peter Cimbolic, Ph.D. is Director of the Counseling Center at The Catholic University of America, where he is also Associate Professor of Psychology and teaches in the Clinical Psychology Doctoral Program. Dr. Cimbolic has published extensively in the area of depression and suicide. He has coauthored with John Hipple one of the most widely used clinical intervention guides, *The Counselor and Suicidal Crisis*, 1979, Charles C Thomas Publisher. He has also coauthored with James M. Corry a comprehensive text on drug use and abuse, *Drugs: Facts, Alternatives, Decisions*, 1985, Wadsworth Publishing Company.

James R. Eyman, Ph.D. is a staff psychologist as well as Director of Suicide Research at the Menniger Clinic in Topeka, Kansas. Dr. Eyman is an active researcher and author in the field of suicidology and is the cochair of the Risk Assessment Committee of the American Association of Suicidology. Dr. Eyman is also on the faculty of the Karl Menninger School of Psychiatry and Mental Health Sciences.

Susanne Kohn Eyman, Ph.D. is in private practice at Mental Health Associates in Manhattan, Kansas. She has published in the areas of suicide, psychological assessment and sexual dysfunction.

Kimberly R. Hamrick, M.P.H. is a Research and Development Associate for the Education Development Center (EDC). Ms. Hamrick has experience in developing health education curricula and is currently helping revise a comprehensive school-based primary prevention program for adolescents. She has a special interest in injury prevention and has worked on several projects related to preventing both intentional and unintentional injuries.

David A. Jobes, Ph.D. is an Assistant Professor of Psychology and member of the Clinical Faculty at The Catholic University of America. He is also the Director of Training and a staff clinician at the university's Counseling Center. Dr. Jobes has actively conducted research and published in the field of suicidology. In addition, Dr. Jobes has conducted numerous training seminars on suicide risk assessment, has served as a clinical consultant to crisis hotlines, and has provided research consultation to the Centers for Disease Control.

Cheryl J. Vince, M.A. is Vice President and Director of School and Society Programs for the Education Development Center (EDC). Ms. Vince has expertise in designing health education programs for schools and community agencies. EDC has worked extensively with schools nationwide to assess their needs and train teachers to use comprehensive school health curricula. Ms Vince has a special interest in preventing injuries to young people, including unintentional (such as motor vehicle crashes) and intentional injuries (such as suicide and violence).

Ellen S. Zinner, Psy.D. is a Certified Death Educator, Grief Counselor, and Lecturer with extensive professional experience in the areas of death, dying, and survivorship. Dr. Zinner has worked directly with survivors of suicide, consulted, given workshops, and written widely on death-related topics. Dr. Zinner is Vice President of the Association for Death Education and Counseling. She is an Assistant Professor in the Department of Psychology at Frostburg State University, Frostburg, Maryland.

*To my uncle, Stephen Cimbolic, who has been like a brother,
a father, and is always a friend.*
       PC

To my parents, Frank and Helen, and Colleen.
       DAJ

PREFACE

Youth suicide has increased dramatically over the last thirty-five years. Depending on the subgroup under examination, suicide is now the second or third leading cause of death in young people between the ages of fifteen and twenty-four years. Clearly, the emotional impact of these losses is tremendous. While many of us think of being young as a carefree time of little responsibility, the fact remains that young people are killing themselves at alarmingly high rates. In recent years the media has brought attention to this increase, but this coverage has often resulted in hyperbole and a distortion of the facts. We would therefore like to present in this book the problem of youth suicide in a balanced, factual manner, using both empirical and clinical data. As much as possible, we have interspersed specific suggestions we have found useful as experienced clinicians.

To begin our discussion, we are going to first explore the basic scope of the problem from an epidemiological, demographic, and sociocultural perspective. For example, we will examine the changing patterns of those at risk for suicide by age, gender, and method over the last twenty years. Having considered suicide first from a general perspective, we will then review issues of suicide risk assessment in youth by considering the difficulties in trying to "predict" an extremely low base-rate event like suicide.

Our discussion of assessment begins with "objective" paper-and-pencil self-report instruments. An examination of their validity and reliability as it relates to suicide risk will be considered and what they may add to the precision in this science/art of clinical assessment. The assessment focus will shift somewhat as we consider the clinical/diagnostic interview as it specifically applies to the assessment of suicidal risk. Discussion of the various interview tools and techniques of assessment will be presented which can be integrated to obtain information which will lead to the best overall global index of suicide risk at a particular point in time. We feel strongly that the appropriate assessment of suicide should not, or cannot, be limited to one discrete assessment procedure at one moment in time, since competent assessment of suicide requires a variety of data obtained in an ongoing process. Clinicians often find that those who were not at risk when initially evaluated may become suicidal later, while the converse could be true as well. In that vein, we shall stress that the delineation between suicide assessment and intervention is an obscure (if not impossible) distinction to make. Therefore, our subsequent discussion of treatment is closely intertwined with ongoing assessment of risk.

We realize that in dealing with potential suicide victims in either assessment or treatment ethical and legal dilemmas confront the "helper." In working with minors these issues become even more complex. Therein we will try to provide the reader some perspective to the various forces that come into play from a legal and ethical perspective and how these impact the person in the helper/assessor role.

The focus will then shift as we consider "special issues" unique to youth suicide which have not been as extensively addressed in the literature. The first of these issues centers on aftermath of suicide — those issues which confront those who survive a youthful suicide. While the pain associated with any death may seem unbearable, survivorship is that much more accentuated when the victim is a young person who dies by their own hand. Often, the survivors of youth suicide are ignored in their communities and frankly in the suicide literature (until more recently). To more fully address this topic, a chapter will focus specifically on this forgotten constituency.

Imitative (modelling) effects of suicide, the "Werther effect," and the occurrence of suicide "clusters" is another set of special issues which has received a great deal of recent attention. We will discuss both the relevant history and empirical data which bear on the evolution of thinking related to these phenomena.

A final issue we will explore is that of school-based suicide prevention (curriculum) programming. While intuitively appealing, the scant research conducted on such programming has provided some mixed results. In our final chapter we will present the inherent issues and recommendations related to the role and scope of suicide education as a means of suicide prevention within secondary education.

P.C.
D.A.J.

ACKNOWLEDGEMENTS

We would like to acknowledge and thank key people who helped make this book possible. We deeply appreciate the contributions of each of our contributing authors whose expertise and extensive work through successive drafts led to the successful completion of this manuscript. Their responsiveness, flexibility, and patience has been most appreciated. A special thanks goes to David Missar and Honora Price-Laszlo whose professional, competent, and tireless efforts, particularly in the final stages of preparation, were instrumental in making this book possible. We would like to thank Father Bob Friday, Vice President for Student Life at The Catholic University of America, for his support in our writing of this book. Finally, we would like to thank our publisher Charles C Thomas, and Mr. Payne Thomas in particular, for making the publication of this book possible.

CONTENTS

YOUTH SUICIDE

Chapter 1

YOUTH SUICIDE: THE SCOPE OF THE PROBLEM

Peter Cimbolic, Ph.D. and David A. Jobes, Ph.D.

Introduction

Over the past ten years there has been a significant increase in the public's awareness of youth suicide. Much of this recent awareness has come from extensive (and at times sensational) media coverage. Understandably, parents, educators, and mental health professionals have responded strongly to the problem, as reflected in widespread development of suicide education programming (see Chap. 6,) and the notable increase in the empirical research devoted to the topic (Berman & Tanney, 1984). As the problem of youth suicide tends to touch deep emotional chords within all of us, it is important to understand the actual shifts in the data base of this phenomena to separate the smoke from the fire. As Berman (1987) noted, misrepresentation and distortion of the data by the media and even among those presenting themselves as "experts" is not unusual.

What may be surprising is that youth suicide is not a new social health crisis. Indeed, almost 80 years ago Sigmund Freud and the Vienna Psychoanalytic Society addressed the significant public health issue of alarming increases in student suicides in the year 1910 (Berman, 1986). Epidemiologists (e.g. Holinger, 1978; Holinger & Offer, 1981) who regularly use mortality statistics to track suicide trends find that rates meaningfully fluctuate over time. For various subgroups, including youthful populations, suicide as a cause of death increases and decreases over the decades.

While the preceding places today's concern about youth suicide in historical context, it is not meant to minimize current concerns about the scope of the problem, as modern-day youth suicide is a tragic, serious, and alarming problem. It is, however, essential that the true scope of the problem be realistically understood. Our examination of youth suicide then begins with a look at the most basic actuarial data. We first present an overview of the extent of suicide in our culture, followed by a more specific examination of suicidal vulnerability as a function of the variables of sex, race, and age and changes in suicide methods over time and to the present day.

Suicide as a Cause of Death

Within this century, there have been notable changes in the causes of death in the United States. According to the National Center for Health Statistics, Division of Vital Statistics, National Vital Statistics System (1988), of the ten leading causes of death in 1900, five of the ten were due to infectious disease. Not surprisingly, suicide did not appear within these ten leading causes of death. However by 1950, following significant medical breakthroughs in disease control, there were only two infectious diseases within the ten leading causes of death. Suicide by then had become the tenth leading cause of death. By 1988, heart disease and cancer accounted for almost 60 percent of all deaths while suicide was the eighth leading cause of death in the general population. The movement of suicide from tenth to eighth reflects the decrease of other causes rather than a meaningful increase in the suicide rate. Over the past 35 years the overall suicide rate has been a remarkably stable statistic—the suicide rate per 100,000 resident population in 1950 was 11.0, by 1960 it had dropped to 10.6 per 100,000 resident population, by 1980 it was up to 11.4, and in 1985 it was 11.5 per resident population.

Considering that the overall suicide rate has been relatively stable, one might wonder why there has been such a national focus on suicide, particularly youth suicide, in recent years? To better understand the shift over time an examination of the data and the specific variables (such as sex, race, marital status, age, and method) that help illuminate the true nature of changes and trends for suicidal deaths will be helpful.

Race and Gender as Variables

Some striking trends become apparent when race and gender are taken into consideration. For white males over the past 35 years, suicide appears to be relatively stable, in that there were 18.1 suicide deaths per 100,000 resident population in 1950 as compared to 20.1 in 1987 (reflecting approximately a 10% increase). Over the same time span, there was a notable increase in suicide deaths in black males (rising from 7.0 in 1950 to 12.0 per 100,000 in 1987 — a 60% increase). White males, in summary, account for over 70 percent of all suicidal deaths.

Turning to differences in causes of death by gender, some dramatic differences between suicide rates specifically are apparent. Men are strikingly more likely to commit suicide than women. White men are four times more likely to kill themselves than white women, while black men are five times more likely to kill themselves than black women. Interestingly, the suicide rate for white women has not changed in thirty-five years; the rate in 1950 is exactly the same figure in 1985. However, for black women there is a little more fluctuation over this thirty-five-year period as the 1950 rate of 1.7 per 100,000 almost doubled by 1970 to 2.9, only to decrease to 2.1 by 1985.

Age as a Variable

Another predictor variable of suicide is age. For all races and sexes, there is a persistent and clear trend that reflects increased suicide risk as a function of increased age.

Not unexpectedly, white males have the strongest association between age and suicide. This correlation has been consistently strong for the last 35 years, with white males over 75 years old being the age/sex category most at risk for suicide. Initially, this may be a surprising observation. However, upon further reflection it is clear that deaths from natural causes have taken the lives of most of their birth cohorts, in effect, leaving behind the most disease-resistant survivors in this category. Men over 75 in our culture will have lost most of their supports, their "reasons for living" in a culture that is not known for its veneration of the elderly.

The relationship between increased age and increased suicide risk is apparent in other race and sex categories, although the association is much weaker for women and blacks.

Youth Suicide Statistics

The preceding sets the stage for our central interest, youth suicide. Suicide was the third leading cause of death in 1988 for youth aged 15–24. There was a 287 percent increase in suicide for young people between the ages of 15 and 24 between 1959 and 1985. The race/gender group that was most responsible for the major impact of this increase are white males. In 1950 white male suicides between the ages of 15–24 were

6.6 per 100,000 residents, whereas by 1985 there were 22.7 suicide deaths for the same group (a 344% increase). During the same period there were also increases for black males, in that there were 4.9 suicide deaths per 100,000 population in 1950, while the figure rose to 13.3 by 1985, an increase of over 270%.

Once again, the suicide rate comparisons are quite different for young women than men. For white females between the ages of 15–24 the 1950 suicide rate per 100,000 of 2.7 had risen to 4.7 by 1985, a 74 percent increase but still significantly less in comparison to either white or black males. An examination of changes in suicide rates for black women between the ages 15–24 from 1950 to 1985 leads to an intriguing comparison. There has been almost no overall change, with the exception of an unusual fluctuation. The suicide rate for black women rose dramatically from 1950 to 1970, showing over a 200 percent increase; yet, from 1970 to 1985 there was an encouraging reversal of this trend almost back to the 1950 level.

Method and Youth Suicide

Having examined some of the youth suicide trends, it is important to put these statistics in context. Specifically, there has been a dramatic increase in youth suicide in recent years, but it is not only the rate that is changing. What is also changing are the methods being used to complete suicides by the young. One alarming observation is that firearms accounted for about half of completed suicides for males between the ages of 15–24, but by 1980 65 percent of the suicide deaths for males of this age were by gunshot. In a recent empirical investigation it was shown that the availability of firearms was a key factor in differentiating young people who had attempted suicide from those who had actually completed suicide (Brent, Perper, Goldstein, Kolko, Allan, Allman, & Zelenak, 1988). The period from 1970 to 1980 reveals some startling shifts in behavior for young women. For this population, there has been a dramatically decreasing trend line for suicide by poison (solid and liquid), usually by drug overdose. In 1970 about 43 percent of the suicides were by drug overdose, whereas in 1980 only slightly more than 20 percent of suicidal deaths were by overdose. However, in an almost mirror-opposite relationship, suicide by gunshot has increased dramatically for young women. In 1970 the method of firearms accounted for slightly more than 30 percent of youthful female suicide deaths, but by 1980 suicide by gunshot accounted for almost 55 percent of these suicidal deaths. This increased use of guns by young women is alarming, since one important component in assessing suicidal risk involves an assessment of potential reversibility of a method used in an attempt (see Chap. 3). One of the reasons that the completed suicide rate for males is, and has been, so much higher when compared to females is that males have tended to use less reversible methods, particularly gunshot. Similarly, the shift by women using more lethal methods may significantly change the emerging profile of youthful suicide in women.

Such trends are meaningful to researchers, mental health practitioners, public health officials, and ultimately the general public. The rapid increase of use of firearms by women or the threefold increase in youth suicide since 1950 are examples of statistical trends which are important to track in research, how they should affect public health policy, and subsequently in prevention programming. Indeed, the statistical trends in youth suicide have directly led to the development of a federal public health policy objective by the Department of Health and Human Services to decrease youth suicide by 1990 (Centers for Disease Control, 1985). While it is important to attend to the statistics, we may only be seeing the tip of the youth suicide iceberg. Much has been written about the suspected underreporting of suicide as an officially reported death statistic, especially among youth (see Jobes, Berman, & Josselson, 1987). The actual magnitude of the youth suicide problem may be greatly underestimated.

Summary

This chapter examined the most basic data used in suicide research and prevention, namely, suicide mortality statistics. To provide a factual foundation for our focus on youth suicide, we examined the changes in suicide as a cause of death and those variables that predict risk. While the overall suicide rate in the United States has remained relatively stable, there have been shifts in who is at risk. While white males (especially above 75) are the most at risk, the dramatic tripling of suicide among all youth 15–24 since 1950 is alarming. Having examined the facts, the focus turns to youth suicide assessment, treatment, and special issues.

References

Berman, A. L. & Tanney, B. (1984). Taking the mystery out of research. Paper presented at the annual meeting of the American Association of Suicidology, Anchorage, Alaska.

Berman, A. L. (1986). A critical look at our adolescence: Notes on turning 18 (and 75). *Suicide and Life-Threatening Behavior, 16,* 1–12.

Berman, A. L. (1987). The reporting of youth suicide statistics. *Newlink.*

Brent, D., & Kolko, D. Risk factors for adolescent suicide. *Archives of General Psychiatry, 45*(6), 581–588.

Brent, D. A., Perper, J. A., Goldstein, C. E., Kolko, D. J., Allan, M. J., Allman, C. J., & Zelenak, J. P. (1988). Risk factors for adolescent suicide: A comparison of adolescent suicide victims with suicidal inpatients. *Archives of General Psychiatry, 45,* 581–588.

Centers for Disease Control: Suicide Surveillance, 1970–1980. Issued April 1985, pp. 26, 31.

Holinger, P. C. (1978). Adolescent suicide: An epidemiological study of recent trends. *American Journal of Psychiatry, 135,* 754–756.

Holinger, P. C., & Offer, D. (1981). Perspectives on suicide in adolescence. *Research in Community and Mental Health, 2,* 139–157.

Jobes, D. A., Berman, A. C., & Josselson, A. R. (1987). Improving the validity and reliability of medical-legal certifications of suicide. *Suicide and Life-Threatening Behavior, 17,* 310–324.

National Center for Health Statistics: *Health, United States, 1987.* DHHS Pub. No. (PHS)88-1232. Public Health Service. Washington. U.S. Government Printing Office, Mar. 1988, pp. 10 & 11.

Chapter 2

SUICIDE RISK AND ASSESSMENT INSTRUMENTS

James R. Eyman, Ph.D.[1] *and Susanne Kohn Eyman, Ph.D.*[2]

Introduction

The purpose of suicide assessment is to be able to identify those at risk and to intervene in a timely fashion. The use of assessment instruments can be extremely valuable to clinicians, if they provide more or different information than can be obtained through an interview, or provide it more efficiently. For example, a paper-and-pencil inventory could be administered to large groups of adolescents, identifying those under stress or experiencing more than usual difficulty with depression or suicidal ideation. This would not be possible through interviews, given limited time and resources. Also, individuals who had difficulty articulating directly their concerns about suicide might be more able to reveal this through testing.

Despite these advantages, it is unfortunately quite difficult to develop useful tests to assess suicidal thoughts and risk. Psychologists have had little success predicting any behavior, let alone a behavior like suicide, which occurs very infrequently and which is multiply determined. Nevertheless, the tragedy of suicide demands every attempt to increase our skill in its prediction. Any instrument, to be helpful, must first consistently measure the phenomenon, either through agreement among items on a paper-and-pencil measure or by being able to be scored similarly by different raters. Certain types of reliability, such as test-retest, might not be as important when measuring less enduring aspects of suicidality, such as depression or hopelessness, but might be crucial when assessing long-standing characterological features that might lead to a suicidal life course. Criterion or predictive validity, while elusive, is critical in this field. It is particularly important to have a very low false

1. The Menninger Clinic, Topeka Kansas
2. Mental Health Associates, Manhattan, Kansas

9

negative rate; that is, predicting that an individual will not be suicidal when, in fact, they are. A thorough review of the difficulties that arise when constructing instruments to predict suicide risk is found in a chapter by Eyman, Mikawa, and Eyman (1990). In presenting the instruments in this chapter, we have attempted to provide the reader with information about these important characteristics. The goal of using psychological instruments to provide efficient, useful, and alternative information about suicide risk has evolved along two lines: (a) the use of existing psychological tests (e.g., the Rorschach, MMPI, or TAT) to assess suicide potential; and (b) the construction of psychological instruments to assess suicide potential. Unfortunately (with a few exceptions), efforts to use existing tests to assess suicide have not provided applications which prove to have valid or reliable predictive utility (see Lester, 1970; Eyman et al., 1989). Alternatively, efforts to construct suicide-specific instruments show somewhat more promise but have significant limitations as well. Ironically, while a great deal has been written about the use of psychological tests to assess suicide, relatively little has been written about suicide-specific instruments. Therefore, our focus in the present chapter will center on the various instruments which have been constructed to predict suicide risk. Before proceeding it is important to note that relatively few instruments have been constructed for a suicidal adolescent population. We have therefore also reviewed the instruments most commonly used with adults as they may be appropriate for use with younger populations. We hope further research will demonstrate the effectiveness of these instruments with an adolescent population.

In writing this chapter, the authors assume that the readers have adequate training in the proper use of psychological tests. While this chapter contains information of interest for both the beginning and experienced practitioner, psychological tests should only be used by those individuals who are able to evaluate the appropriateness of the instrument for the task and who are appropriately trained to interpret the results.

Scales to Predict Suicidal Behavior

Hilson Adolescent Profile

Inwald, Brobst, and Morissey (1987) developed the Hilson Adolescent Profile (HAP) as a screening tool for adolescent behavior problems. The profile contains 310 true and false items, constructed on a rational-intuitive basis, divided into 16 scales: guarded response, alcohol use, drug use, educational adjustment difficulties, law/society violations, frustration tolerance, antisocial risktaking, rigidity/obsessiveness, inter-personal/assertiveness difficulties, home life conflicts, social/sexual adjustment, health concerns, anxiety/phobia avoidance, suspicious temperament, depression/suicide potential, and unusual responses. A manual contains normative data for 2,259 adolescents divided into three groups: juvenile offenders, clinical inpatients and outpatients, and a school population. The instrument is computer scored.

The Depression/Suicide Scale had an acceptable internal consistency of .88, and test-retest reliability measured over a two- to four-week period on a sample of students was quite good at .92. Forty-nine high school adolescents who had made at least one suicide attempt were compared to 379 students who had made no attempts, using a stepwise discriminant analysis. The suicide attempters scored significantly higher on alcohol use, educational adjustment difficulties, law/society violations, frustration tolerance, rigidity/obsessiveness, social/school adjustment, anxiety/phobic avoidance, suspicious temperament, and depression/suicide potential. Seventy-two percent of those who had not made an attempt were correctly classified, as were 74 percent of the adolescents who had attempted suicide, although the manual is not clear as to how the classification was accomplished, i.e. using a cutoff score or other criterion. Seventy-nine percent of juvenile offenders who never made a suicide attempt were correctly classified, as were 91 percent of offenders who had made at least one attempt. For the clinical population, the correct classifications were 74 percent and 67 percent, respectively.

The HAP was factor analyzed, with a resulting three factors which accounted for a total of 64 percent of the variance. The depression/suicide potential scale loaded on both the first (internalized problems) and third (depression, worry, and low self-esteem) factors. There is no information available on item-to-total score correlations, nor is there information regarding the unique variance of each scale. Thus, it cannot be determined that the scales are measuring distinct, unrelated concepts.

The HAP is promising in its ability to distinguish suicidal and non-suicidal adolescents in school and offender populations. Unfortunately, in a clinical population, the misclassification of one-third of suicide attempters would be dangerous, particularly if the instrument was relied on solely. Another problem is the construction of the depression/suicide scale, which is heavily oriented toward the assessment of depressive affect. Perhaps the high false positive rate results from a confounding of depressed and suicidal adolescents, which could happen easily in a clinical population.

Suicide Probability Scale

The Suicide Probability Scale (SPS) by Cull and Gill (1986) was designed for use with adults and adolescents. It is unique both in design and construction, combining theoretical and empirical approaches. Items were generated based on Durkheim's concept of anomie, Freud's conceptualization of introjected rage, Shneidman's ideas about perturbation, and the notion of impulsive action and constricted cognitive style.

Respondents are asked to rate the frequency of occurrence for thirty-six items using Likert scales ranging from "none or a little of the time" to "most or all of the time." However, given the structure of the instrument, it is not clear whether the responses refer to current or past experiences. Two global scores are obtained: a normalized total T-score, and a suicide probability score which is the statistical likelihood that an individual might belong in a population of lethal suicide attempters. The suicide probability is determined based on the context in which the person is being assessed: high risk for those using a suicide prevention center or for psychiatric inpatients, intermediate risk for those in an outpatient setting, and low risk for the general population. In addition to the global scores, four subscale scores are obtained: hopelessness, suicide ideation, negative self-evaluation, and hostility.

Internal consistency coefficients ranged from .62 for the negative self-evaluation scale to .93 for the total score, similar to the split-half reliability, which ranged from .58 for negative self-evaluation to .93 for total score. All the coefficients except that for negative self-evaluation are acceptable. Factor analysis indicated that the scale items were scattered among the factors (Golding, 1985) and scales were intercorrelated above .70. Thus, the subscales are not statistically sound, nor independent, and should be used with caution.

Discriminant function analysis correctly classified approximately 85% of individuals as suicidal or non-suicidal. However, employing differential cutting scores based on the three presumptive risk categories (mild, moderate, severe) the false negative rate was 2 percent in the high risk group, 17 percent in the intermediate risk group, and 71 percent in the low risk group. This misclassification rate among the low risk group makes the scale of questionable clinical utility.

The "presumed risk" notion is problematic. The individual's "risk" for suicide is determined by the setting, before the instrument is administered. Why, then, is a screening device necessary? For those in the low risk category, screening would be most useful; however, in this group the misclassification rate is 71 percent (Eyman, Mikawa, & Eyman, 1990). Furthermore, separate norms are unavailable for adolescents. Research and clinical evidence points to differences between adolescents and adults who make serious suicide attempts, so that adult norms might be inappropriate for teenagers (Eyman, Mikawa, & Eyman, 1990).

Index of Potential Suicide

The Index of Potential Suicide (IPS) (Zung, 1974) measures potential suicide risk and includes social-demographic and clinical variables that were selected from previous suicide scales. The social-demographic variables include demographic status, socioeconomic status, environmental stress, family history and past medical history. The clinical variables measure alcoholism, anxiety, current general health, depression, emotional status, and suicidal behavior. Depression is rated by the Zung Depression Scale (Zung, 1965), and the scale Zung (1971) developed to rate anxiety disorders comprises the anxiety measure. Zung investigated the IPS using a group of psychiatric inpatients. The demographic portion of the IPS did not distinguish between those patients who had no suicidal behavior, had suicidal ideations, made a suicide threat, or attempted suicide; however, the clinical variables were able to do so.

Crisis intervention volunteers and non-volunteer subjects were administered the Index of Potential Suicide (Zung and Moore, 1976). In all the clinical categories except alcoholism, there was a trend of increasing scores with degree of suicidal behavior (no suicidal behavior, ruminators, threateners, and attempters). T-tests indicated that the non-suicidal group scored significantly lower on all the clinical items, except alcoholism, as compared to the suicidal group (ruminators, threateners, and attempters). When the scores of the subjects with a history of suicidal behavior were compared to the scores of inpatient psychiatric subjects in a previous study (Zung, 1974), the psychiatric patients scored significantly higher on measures of depression, anxiety, alcoholism, and concerns about current health. The results indicate the need to have separate norms for different populations.

Moore, Judd, Zung, and Alexander (1979) found that the subjects who had made a suicide attempt scored higher on the Index of Potential Suicide than subjects who had made no attempt. Petrie and Chamberlain (1985) investigated the ability of the Index of Potential Suicide to predict future suicidal behavior by administering the IPS to patients who attempted suicide within two days of their suicide attempt. Six months after the attempt, the subjects were sent a questionnaire seeking information about their suicidal behavior over the past six months. Sixty-nine percent of the subjects completed and returned the follow-up questionnaire. Using this group of subjects, the internal consistency coefficient for the clinical scale was .84, .75 for the depression subscale, emotional status—.70, anxiety—.69, suicidal behavior—.59, alcoholism—.55, and general health—.38, indicating that the suicidal behavior, alcoholism, and general health subscale have questionable internal consistency. Concurrent validity was investigated by correlating each subscale with suicidal ideation and number of prior suicide attempts. Depression and emotional status were significantly correlated with suicidal ideation and number of prior suicide attempts. The anxiety subscale was significantly correlated to suicidal ideation but not to prior attempts. None of the clinical subscales were significantly correlated with number of suicide attempts within the six-month follow-up. The IPS seems to be able to adequately distinguish between individuals with no suicidal behavior and those with past and present suicidal behavior/ideation, and may therefore have some clinical utility.

Scale for Assessing Suicide Risk (SASR)

In an attempt to answer another important question in suicide prediction, Tuckman and Youngman (1968) developed a Scale for Assessing Suicide Risk to identify among suicide attempters those individuals with a high potential to commit suicide. They evaluated risk factors involved in suicide attempts by persons ages 18 and older of which 48 were completed suicides. Answers to each factor were conceptually divided into high risk and low risk categories. For example, one of the factors was age, with 45 years of age or older considered high risk category, while 45 years of age and under was low risk. Based on the samples studied, the suicide rate per 1,000 population among the high and low risk categories were established and 17 factors differentiated between high and low risk. A total score of 17 is possible, as one point is given for each high risk factor present. The authors concluded that the higher the SASR score, the higher the suicide rate. The predictive ability of the SASR was investigated by Resnick and Kendra (1973) using 63 psychiatric patients who attempted suicide and 25 psychiatric patients who completed suicide. Suicide rates in the high risk and low risk category for each of the 17 variables were calculated as in the Tuckman and Youngman study, but only 7 variables were found to be consistent with previous studies—age 45 or older, male, unemployed, poor emotional condition, methods of hanging, jumping, firearms, or drowning, attempt during warm months, and self-reported suicidal intent. The authors also found that an increasing risk score surprisingly corresponded to a decreasing suicide completion rate. Resnick and Kendra conclude that the SASR is not applicable to a psychiatric population but might be valuable in a non-psychiatric population as used by Tuckman and Youngman. We agree that the scale should not be used for a psychiatric population and also believe its use in a general population is premature, as the original finding has not been replicated.

Scale to Predict Future Suicide in Individuals Who Have Attempted Suicide

Pallis, Barraclough, Levey, Jenkins, and Sainsbury (1982) reasoned that the risk of future suicide among suicide attempters would be greatest among the attempters who had characteristics most similar to individuals who completed suicide. They collected information on the personal and social characteristics of 151 patients who made a suicide attempt and 75 individuals who committed suicide. Differences between the groups were examined using a stepwise discriminate analysis, and of the 203 items that were coded 20 significantly discriminated between the two groups. Of these 20 items, seven were chosen for a shorter scale. Using the seven-item scale and weighted scores, a score of 28.5, four out of five suicides scored at or above this point and four out of five attempters below this point. The 20-item scale using weighted score found that the score of 87 provided optimal discrimination between the two groups. Pallis, Gibbons, and Pierce (1984) concluded that the 20-item scale in combination with a measure of suicide intent was the most accurate predictor of future suicidal behavior. This is a promising scale whose theoretical premise is sound. However, the scale needs to be revalidated on a new subject pool because the very good discriminant ability of the scale might be capitalizing on chance. It also remains to be seen as to whether its discriminant validity is maintained for an adolescent/young adult clientele.

Suicide Potential Scale

The Suicide Potential Scale was initially developed by Miskimins, DeCook, Wilson, and Maley (1967) to predict which psychiatric patients were vulnerable to committing suicide. The scale was developed by constructing items and establishing through discriminate analysis those items which differentiated between 16 psychiatric patients who had committed suicide and non-suicidal patients matched for sex, age, marital status, and diagnosis. Twenty-three items were found to differentiate between the two groups and three additional items were added to the scale. Miskimins and Wilson (1969) administered the Suicide Potential Scale to 15 psychiatric patients who subsequently committed suicide and 30 non-suicidal patients. An item analysis was conducted to eliminate those items that did not differentiate between the two groups. Ten items were eliminated and the 16 remaining items became the Revised Suicide Potential Scale (RSPS). Subjects from the two studies were pooled and the suicidal patients had significantly higher mean scores than the non-suicidal patients. Braucht and Wilson (1970) investigated the RSPS scores of 63 patients who committed suicide, 324 who attempted suicide, and 95 non-suicidal control patients. The RSPS correctly classified 58 percent of the patients. However, this classification is spuriously high because some of the patients in this group were those on which the scale was initially developed. Based on the poor classification results, the Suicide Potential Scale's use in a clinical setting cannot be recommended.

A Scale for Predicting Subsequent Suicidal Behavior

Buglass and McCulloch (1970) developed scales to predict further suicidal behavior, after examining patients who repeated a suicide attempt or committed suicide within a three-year period after being admitted following a drug overdose. Out of 34 items assessed initially at admission, three items were significantly associated with repetition of suicidal behavior in males. They were violence in key relationships, a diagnosis of alcoholism, and having taken alcohol at the time of a suicide attempt. For females, nine items were significantly related to repetition of suicidal behavior: previous attempted suicide, previous psychiatric treatment, psychopathy, drug addiction, four or more residence changes in the past five years, father absent when patient was under ten years of age, poor work record, and violence in key relationships. In general, the more items endorsed, the greater the correct classification of repetition. For example, 57 percent of those males who repeated a suicidal gesture had all three items present. Similarly, 52 percent of the females who repeated a suicide attempt had six or seven of the variables present. In a validation study on a sample of patients who repeated suicidal behavior over a one-year period, the authors concluded that the female scale was valid but that the male scale did not have enough predictive validity to warrant its continued use. Subsequently, Chowdhury, Hicks and Kreitman (1973) reached the same conclusion. Caution is further urged in the use of the female scale, in that it was not developed on a "young" sample.

Scales to Measure Suicidal Ideation

The exact relationship between suicidal ideation and actual suicidal behavior remains elusive. While an ideator may never attempt, it is probably rare that an attempter is not an ideator. Accordingly, this logic has led a number of investigators to construct instruments which measure suicidal ideation.

Scale for Suicide Ideation (SSIr Ideators)

Scale for Suicide Ideation (SSI) was designed by Beck, Kovacs, and Weissman (1979) to quantify the intensity of current conscious suicidal intent. A 30-item scale was administered to suicidal patients, and items that overlapped, were confusing, or difficult to score were eliminated resulting in the current 19-item scale. Each item has three alternative statements scored from zero to two, and the total score is calculated by adding the individual item scores for a possible range of scores from zero to 38. The SSI has five subscales: (1) characteristics of attitude toward living and dying, (2) characteristics of suicide ideation or wish, (3) characteristics of contemplated attempt, (4) actualization of contemplated attempt, and (5) background factors. The SSI is an interview instrument.

Internal consistency of this scale was assessed through item-to-total score correlations on a sample of patients who were hospitalized for self-destructive ruminations. Internal consistency was a robust .89. The items were all positively correlated with the total and ranged from .04 to .72 with a median correlation of .51. Twenty-five of the 90 patients were rated by two different clinicians for an interrater reliability of .83.

Concurrent validity was determined by correlating the ideation score with the self-harm item on the Beck Depression Inventory and was .41. The author observes that this low correlation may be an artifact of the limited range on the Beck Depression Inventory item (0 to 3). Discriminant validity was assessed by comparing the scores of the 90 patients hospitalized for suicidal ideation with 50 outpatients who sought psychiatric treatment for depression but were not suicidal. A T-test yielded a significant difference between the groups even though the two groups had similar BDI scores. Thus, the SSI discriminated between groups differing in degree of suicidal intent.

A factor analysis yielded three distinct factors. Factor 1 accounted for 35 percent of the variance and was labeled "Active Suicidal Desire" and was made up of ten items. Factor 2, "Preparation," included three items and accounted for approximately 11 percent of the variance. Factor 3, "Passive Suicidal Desire," was made up of three items and accounted for approximately 10 percent of the variance.

Holden, Mendonca, and Mazmanian (1985) administered the SSI to hospitalized suicide ideators and factor analyzed the scale. A forced 3-factor solution was not supported using Horn's (1965) criterion for the underlying factor structure. However, a two-factor solution was derived with factor 1, labelled "Suicidal Desire" containing nine items and accounting for approximately 25 percent of the variance, while factor 2, "Suicide Preparation," contained nine items and accounted for 17 percent of the variance. Not surprisingly, this second factor contained most of the items which had previously been found in Beck's second and third factor.

Miller, Norman, Bishop, and Dow (1986) further modified the Scale for Suicide Ideation by (1) adding standardized prompt questions, (2) standardizing the sequence of administration, (3) modifying the ratings points to increase specificity in range, (4) developing initial screening scores, and (5) selecting further items for inclusion in this scale. The Modified Scale for Suicide Ideation (MSSI) contains 25 items. The scale is composed of 18 of the 19 original SSI items, two additional items that resulted from dividing an original SSI item into two items, and three additional items (intensity of suicidal thoughts, talk of death, and writing of death).

The first four items were designated as screening items and were found to have acceptable internal consistency of .86 and item-to-total correlations ranging from .57 to .79, using 113 hospitalized patients with a diagnosis of a major depression. The validity of the screening score was assessed by comparing the screening score to clinicians' ratings on 30 suicidal ideators with an agreement between the MSSI screening score and the clinicians' ratings of 73 percent. The false positive rate was 21 percent and the false negative rate was 6 percent. The MSSI was administered to 54 suicidal ideators and the internal consistency of the total scale was quite good, with a coefficient alpha of .94 and item-to-total score correlations ranging from .41 to .83. Concurrent validity was assessed by correlating the MSSI total score with the suicide items from the Beck Depression Inventory ($r = .60$). The construct validity was examined by correlating the MSSI with the BDI ($r = .34$) and the Beck Hopelessness Scale ($r = .42$). In addition, those patients who had identified suicide as a problem had significantly higher MSSI scores than those patients who did not identify suicide as a problem, indicating discriminant validity. This structured interview appears to have utility. However, caution is warranted for its use with youthful populations, since its development was based on adult samples.

Beck, Steer, and Ranieri (1988) modified the SSI into a self-report instrument. The self-report SSI was filled out in a paper-and-pencil study by 30 patients and administered through a computer to 25 patients. The paper-and-pencil administration SSI scores correlated with clinicians' ratings .90. In addition, there was no significant difference between patient means and the psychiatrist mean ratings of the patients. The internal consistency of the paper-and-pencil version was .93. The computerized administration correlated with the clinicians' ratings .94. However, the mean for the computerized and clinically rated SSI were significantly different, with the computerized means being higher. The item-to-total correlations ranged from .54 to .93 and the internal consistency was .97. The SSI appears to be a useful and psychometrically sound instrument in both its interview and self-report form.

Suicidal Ideation Questionnaire

The Suicidal Ideation Questionnaire (SIQ) was developed by Reynolds (1988) to assess adolescents' thoughts about death and suicide. Forms are available for high school and junior high school students (SIQ–JR). Items were derived from data from clinical interviews with depressed adolescents. Interpretation is based on a combination of total score, critical items, and individual patterns. It is suggested that adolescents who score above a cutoff score be evaluated for risk of suicidal behavior. In addition, the author suggests adolescents who endorse three critical items on the SIQ and two on the SIQ–JR be evaluated for suicidal risk. In this manner, the scale becomes used as a screening device for self-destructive behavior, rather than an instrument to assess ideation.

The SIQ manual is well-constructed and contains normative data from 2,180 subjects in grades 7–12. Internal consistency was quite high, with coefficients of .94 for the SIQ–JR and .97 for the SIQ. For the SIQ, item-to-total correlations range from .41 to .84, with a median of .78. The SIQ–JR item-to-total score correlations ranged from .44 to .86, with a median of .75. It may be that a few items should be eliminated from each form. Factor analysis yielded three factors for each form, accounting for a total of .67.7 percent of the variance of the SIQ and 73.3 percent of the variance of the SIQ–JR.

Spirito (1987) administered the SIQ to adolescent suicide attempters shortly after admission to a hospital. Their mean score was 69.6, significantly higher than the mean score of 17.8 in the non-suicidal standardization sample. Approximately two-thirds of the attempters scored above the cutoff score, leaving a false negative rate which is unfortunately probably too high in a clinical setting, particularly if used as the exclusive screening instrument.

Despite the author's claim that the SIQ is "not a diagnostic or predictive measure," the suggested cutoff score changes the use of the instrument. While it is important to know the intensity and components of suicidal ideation, it would also be valuable to obtain data that relates that ideation to the possibility of a suicide attempt. Furthermore, the instrument was developed with a sample of junior and senior high school students. The scores from this general population are most likely inappropriate for adolescent psychiatric patients. Thus, at this time the SIQ may be useful only in a school population (Eyman, Mikawa, and Eyman, 1990).

Scales to Measure Suicidal Intent

The psychological intention inherent in the act of suicide is a central and defining construct. For example, a self-inflicted death can be considered an accident if there was no intention to die. Therefore, some researchers have attempted to measure this construct in hopes of assessing suicide risk.

Suicide Intent Scale (SIS)

The Suicide Intent Scale was developed by Beck, Schuyler, and Herman (1974) to assess the intensity of a person's wish to terminate their life. The SIS excludes indices reflecting the effectiveness of the act. The Suicidal Intent Scale is designed to gather data regarding the intensity of the attempter's wish to die at the time of the attempt. Items were selected from clinical investigations and the literature on suicide.

The scale is divided into three sections and contains 20 items. Each item consists of three alternate statements graded in intensity from zero to two. Only the first two sections, items 1–15, comprise the total score. Information for the recording of the scale is obtained through interview data. The first section, Objective Circumstances Related to the Suicide Attempt, contains items 1–8 and solicits data about the facts of the attempt and events surrounding the attempt such as the "timing" of the suicide attempt and "precautions against discovery." The second section, Self-Report, contains items 9–15 and is used to retrospectively reconstruct the patient's thoughts and feelings at the time of the attempt. These items attempt to reveal the purpose of the attempt, the person's expectations of the fatality of what they had done, and their attitude toward living and dying. The third section, items 16–20, is not scored. It yields data on other aspects of suicide such as risk factors, the individual's current feelings about the suicide attempt, and the role of alcohol.

The Suicide Intent Scale has been found to have an inter-item reliability ranging from .91 (R. Beck, Morris, & A. Beck, 1974) to .95 (A. Beck, Schuyler, & Herman, 1974). Using the data gained from 45 patients who were interviewed soon after a suicide attempt, the SIS was found to have a split-half internal consistency coefficient of .82 (A. Beck, Schuyler, & Herman, 1974). Using 31 patients who made a suicide attempt, the interrater reliability of the SIS was found to be .95 (Minkoff, Bergman, A. Beck, & R. Beck, 1973). To establish construct validity, scores of 31 fatal attempters were compared to the scores of 49 non-fatal attempters. The mean score on the objective circumstances related to the suicide attempt (items 1–8) was significantly higher for the fatal cases (Beck, Schuyler, & Herman, 1974). Similarly, 19 patients who reattempted suicide within one year of discharge from hospitalization had significantly higher scores on the total SIS scale than did 212 attempters who did not reattempt suicide (R. Beck, Morris, & A. Beck, 1974).

A. Beck, Weissman, Lester, and Trexler (1976) obtained data on 188 people who have attempted suicide and factor analyzed the Suicide Intent Scale. Six factors were extracted, including four factors relevant to the first 15 scored items on the scale: (a) "attitudes towards the attempt," accounting for 26 percent of the variance, (b) "planning," accounting for 11 percent of the variance, (c) "precautions against intervention," accounting for 10 percent of the variance, and (d) "communication with others," accounting for 6 percent.

Smith and Eyman (1986) collected data to evaluate section one of the

Suicide Intent Scale, Objective Circumstances Related to Suicide Attempt, on 101 individuals who made suicide attempts. The subjects were grouped into three categories according to the degree of lethality of the attempt, based on the Lethality of Suicide Attempt Rating Scale (Smith, Conroy, & Ehler, 1984). A discriminant function analysis revealed that only three of the first eight SIS items were needed to maximally discriminate among those individuals who made either a mild, moderate, or a serious lethal suicide attempt; "isolation," "precautions against discovery or intervention," and "active preparation for attempt."

Dyer and Kreitman (1984) reviewed the relationship between age, sex, and Suicide Intent Scale score. Contradictory results have been found. Several studies suggest a relationship between age and suicidal intent score (Dyer & Kreitman, 1984; Lester, Beck, & Trexler, 1975; Pierce, 1977), while several studies show no such relationship (Beck, Kovacs, & Weissman, 1975; Goldney, 1979; Minkoff, Bergman, A. Beck, & R. Beck, 1973; Silver, A. Beck, & Marcus, 1971). Pallis (1977) found that the total SIS score was significantly higher for males; however, Lester, Beck, & Trexler (1975) and Dyer and Kreitman (1984) found no relationship by gender.

While there are a few studies that do not support the Suicide Intent Scale's ability to discriminate, this appears to be a psychometrically sound and clinically useful instrument. The scale has very good inter-item reliability, internal consistency, interrater reliability, and validity; thus, it is one of the most promising instruments we have reviewed.

Scales to Measure Hopelessness

The construct of hopelessness has increasingly emerged as a uniquely useful correlate of suicide risk (Beck et al., 1989). This body of literature will, therefore, be summarized as it is thought to relate highly to the prediction of suicidal risk.

Hopelessness Scale

The Hopelessness Scale (HS), developed by Beck, Weissman, Lester, and Trexler (1974), is a 20-item true and false questionnaire that was constructed from both a theoretical and clinical perspective. The twenty items were selected from a test about attitudes towards the future and from pessimistic statements made by psychiatric patients who were judged by clinicians to feel hopeless. The statements selected were felt to reflect different facets of negative attitudes about the future. Using hospitalized patients who had made a recent suicide attempt, the overall internal consistency of the scale was .93. Individual item to total score correlations ranged from a low of .39 (I can't imagine what my life would be like in ten years) to a high of .76 (All I can see ahead of me is unpleasantness rather than pleasantness). The concurrent validity of the HS was investigated using outpatients in a general medical practice and hospitalized patients who had made recent suicide attempts. Correlation of the HS score and clinicians' ratings of the patients' hopelessness in a general practice sample was .74 and in the attempted suicide sample, .62. The interrater reliability was .86. A principle components factor analysis with varimax rotation was calculated on the data supplied by 294 suicide attempters and three factors were obtained accounting for 41 percent, 6 percent, and 5 percent of the variance, respectively. Factor 1 included items labeled "feelings about the future" and were associated with such affects as hope and enthusiasm, happiness, and faith. Factor 2 was labeled "loss of motivation" and loaded on items that concerned giving up. Factor 3, "future expectations," included items regarding anticipation of what life's future will be like.

Several studies have indicated that hopelessness, as measured by the Hopelessness Scale, is a significantly better indicator of suicidal risk than depression, as measured by a number of depression scales. Kovacs, Beck, and Weissman (1975) found hopelessness as measured by the HS, and depression as measured by the Beck Depression Inventory, were both positively correlated with the degree of current suicidal risk as measured by the current Suicidal Intent Scale. Significantly, hopelessness scores showed a significantly higher correlation with current suicidal risk than depression. The partial correlation between depression and current suicidal intent (with hopelessness held constant) was nonsignificant, while the partial correlation between hopelessness and current suicidal intent with depression held constant was significant. This indicates that the relationship between depression and current suicidal intent is probably due to hopelessness as the common source of variance. The hopelessness score was also more highly correlated with the patients' self-evaluation of their will to live than were depression scores. Similarly, Beck, Kovacs, and Weissman (1975), studying hospitalized suicide attempters 17–63 years of age, found that hopelessness was more related to suicide intent as measured by the Suicide Intent Scale than was depression as measured by the BDI. A two-way analysis of variance of suicide intent scores, with high and low hopelessness and high and low depression groups, yielded a significant main effect for hopelessness but not for depression. Partial correlations again confirmed that the relationship between depression and suicidal intent was primarily due to hopelessness. In a parallel finding, clinical evaluations of hopelessness were more closely related to suicidal intent than were clinical evaluations of depression.

Wetzel (1976) administered the BDI, the Hopelessness Scale, and the Zung Depression Scale to emergency room patients. Both hopelessness and depression were significantly greater in suicidal patients. Interestingly, suicide threateners reported significantly more hopelessness than suicide attempters. The hopelessness score showed a significant main effect due to severity of intent, with the high intent group significantly more hopeless, the moderate intent group more hopeless than the low intent group, while the low intent attempters could not be distinguished from a psychiatric non-suicidal control group. Ninety-four subjects were retested at a six-month interval. The direction of change in the hopelessness scores correctly predicted 81 percent of the changes in self-rated suicide risk, while changes in the depression score accounted for 75 percent of the change in self-rated suicide risk. Both hopelessness and depression correlated significantly with suicide intent of the attempters at the time of testing, and when the effect of the other was partialed out, both correlations maintained significance in contrast to the findings of previous studies. Similarly, Wetzel, Margulies, Davis, and Karam (1980) found that among hospitalized psychiatric patients the HS score was significantly more correlated with suicide intent as measured by the SIS than was depression on the MMPI. When the effect of hopelessness was partialed out, there was no relationship between suicide intent and depression. Dyer and Kreitman (1984) administered the SIS, HS, and BDI to subjects ages 15 and older who made a suicide attempt by poisoning and found that the relationship between depression and suicidal intent disappeared when hopelessness was held constant, while the relationship between hopelessness and suicidal intent remained significant when depression was partialed out.

Similarly, three longitudinal studies have indicated that hopelessness as measured by the HS is a constant predictor of suicide among psychiatric patients. Beck, Steer, Kovacs, and Garrison (1985) followed for 5 to 10 years, psychiatric suicide ideators ages 17–65, 14 of whom committed suicide during the follow-up period. Scores on the BDI, the HS, and the

Scale for Suicide Ideation were tabulated on admission and only the Hopelessness Scale significantly differentiated between those suicide ideators who eventually completed suicide over the ten-year period and those who did not. A score of ten or more on the HS correctly identified 91 percent of the suicide completers. The number of true positives above the cutoff score was 11.6 percent and, unfortunately, the number of false positives was 88.4 percent, a very unacceptably high figure.

Two studies, not using the Hopelessness Scale, also found hopelessness to be associated with eventual suicide. Schizophrenic patients who committed suicide during a five-year follow-up period and schizophrenic patients who made suicide attempts during a three- to seven-year follow-up period were studied by Drake, Gates, and Cotton (1986). Hopelessness, as inferred from review of the patients' charts at admission, was found to be significantly greater among the schizophrenic patients who committed suicide as opposed to the schizophrenic patients who made suicide attempts. Similarly, Fawcett, Scheftner, Clark, Hedeker, Gibbons, and Coryell (1987) obtained information from the Schedule for Affective Disorders and Schizophrenia on patients who committed suicide within a four-year period and patients who did not commit suicide. Hopelessness, as measured by the Schedule for Affective Disorders and Schizophrenia, was one of the variables that discriminated significantly between the suicide and non-suicide group.

Unfortunately, the Beck Hopelessness Scale has been used primarily with an adult population. Only a few studies have used an adolescent population. Johnson and McCutcheon (1981) found that for adolescents ages 13–17, Hopelessness Scale scores were significantly correlated with scores on the 13-item short form of the Beck Depression Scale. Suicidal behavior was not investigated in this study. Topol and Reznikoff (1982) obtained Hopelessness Scale scores on hospitalized adolescents who had attempted suicide within three months prior to the study, psychiatric inpatient adolescents, and high school graduates matched for race, age, and socioeconomic status. Hopelessness scores significantly differentiated the suicidal adolescents from the non-suicidal psychiatrically hospitalized adolescents, and the suicidal adolescents were significantly differentiated from the high school graduates.

However, hopelessness as a predictor may be race-specific, in that a recent study in which the Hopelessness Scale was administered to minority female adolescent suicide attempters and a matched group of non-suicidal psychiatric adolescent patients found no difference in level of hopelessness. The author suggested that hopelessness as an indicator of suicide intent among adolescent minority females should be used with caution (Rotheram-Borus & Trautman, 1988).

Hopelessness Scale for Children

The Hopelessness Scale for Children is a 17-item true-and-false inventory that was modeled after Beck's Hopelessness Scale (Kazdin, French, Unis, Esveldt-Dawson, & Sherick, 1983). In administering the scale to acutely disturbed children ages 5–13, Kazdin et al. (1983) found an internal consistency of .75 and item-to-total score correlations that range from a low of .19 to a high of .71.

Encouragingly, the overall hopelessness score was significantly correlated with several measures of depression, including the Children's Depression Inventory, Bellevue Index of Depression, Depression Symptom Checklist, and negatively correlated with the Self-Esteem Inventory. Further, suicidal intent, as defined by either previous suicide attempt or suicidal ideation, positively correlated with the Hopelessness Scale for Children ($r = .35$). Similar to many of the studies using the Beck Hopelessness Scale, the relationship between suicidal intent and depression was lost when hopelessness was partialed out.

Kazdin, Rodgers, and Colbus (1986) administered the Hopelessness Scale for Children to inpatients aged 6–13 and found a very acceptable internal consistency of .97 and a split-half reliability of .96. A factor analysis using a principle-components analysis with varimax rotation yielded two factors accounting for 78 percent of the variance. Unfortunately, the two factors do not make conceptual sense. The authors conclude that based on this factor analysis and the research with the Beck Hopelessness Scale, pessimism about the future and perceived inability to influence outcomes seems to be a powerful common factor in both child, adolescent, and adult hopelessness (Kazdin et al., 1986). Although this is a fairly psychometrically sound scale, the instrument has not been used with a suicidal adolescent population and the relationship between hopelessness as measured by this scale and suicidal behavior is not known, and therefore it has to be used cautiously until more work is done on its validation.

Scales to Measure Lethality of a Suicide Attempt

One way to evaluate the eventual threat to life that a person's suicidal feelings pose is to review the lethality of the attempt, if one has been made. This is certainly not "foolproof" but is probably helpful. We will now review those measures that have been developed to evaluate the "lethality" of suicide attempts.

Risk-Rescue Rating Scale

As past behavior is one of the best predictors of future behavior, it's often valuable to assess the history of previous suicide behavior and the relative lethality of an attempt. In this vein, two major instruments have been developed.

A scale to measure the lethality of a suicide attempt was developed by Weissman and Worden (1974). The Risk-Rescue Rating Scale is based on a compilation of observable risk- and rescue-related factors. Five variables assess the risk that went into a suicide attempt: what type of method was used, state of consciousness during the time of the rescue, lesions and toxicity, degree of medical recovery, and treatment required. The five rescue factors include: the location of the attempt, the person initiating a rescue, probability of discovery, accessibility to rescue, and the delay until discovery. Each of the risk and rescue factors is rated on a scale of one to three and then converted to an overall risk score and an overall rescue score. A total risk-rescue score is computed by a formula developed by the authors. Using subjects who were seen in a hospital for a suicidal behavior, the total risk-rescue rating discriminated significantly between those subjects who committed suicide and those who attempted suicide and did so better than either the risk or rescue rating alone. The interrater reliability was found to be acceptable. This is a promising scale, particularly for use in an inpatient setting to determine eventual lethality.

Lethality of Suicide Attempt Rating Scale (LSARS)

Another scale to measure the level of lethality in a suicide attempt is an 11-point scale developed by Smith, Conroy, and Ehler (1984). The lethality of intent and lethality of method scales developed by McEvoy (1974) were combined to form the Lethality of Suicide Attempt Rating Scale. The scale points were found to differ significantly from each other, suggesting that each scale point represents different perceived levels of lethality as rated by 24 experienced clinicians. Overall interrater reliability for individual raters was found to be .85. Each scale point has examples of suicide attempts and the scale ranges from 0 (death is an impossible result of the suicidal behavior) to 10 (death is almost a certainty regardless of the circumstances or interventions by an outside agent). Most of the people at this level die quickly after the attempt. An appendix of lethal dosages of various medications accompanies this scale.

Conclusion

Prediction of suicide is fraught with difficulties, partly because of the low base rate of the behavior and because the behavior is so multiply determined. Nevertheless, considerable progress has been made toward the development of dependable instruments for the assessment of suicidality, including evaluation of lethality and prediction of risk.

Based on our review, the Scale for Suicide Ideation, the Suicide Intent Scale, and the Hopelessness Scale are recommended for clinical use. With an adolescent population, the Hilson Adolescent Profile can be used with a school and juvenile delinquent population, and the Suicidal Ideation Questionnaire is appropriate with a school population. However, neither scale is recommended for clinical use with psychiatric adolescents. A few tests look promising, including the Scale for Assessing Suicide Risk, the Scale to Predict Suicide in Individuals Who Have Attempted Suicide, and the Hopelessness Scale for Children, but each needs further research to establish their validity. None of the tests currently available should be relied on exclusively to assess suicidality. Information obtained from these instruments must be corroborated by other data sources such as clinical interviews with the patient and appropriate family members, in-depth history, and other psychological tests as appropriate.

What is needed in the area of assessment is to refine our understanding of the phenomena of youth suicide. Early works lumped together individuals who had suicidal ideation, made mild attempts, and those who actually committed suicide. It is now clear that those groups have different characteristics, as do adults and adolescents and males and females. Ideally, tests have to be developed which are oriented to these separate groups.

Even with more specific, reliable, and valid instruments it may remain an impossible task to predict who will engage in suicidal behavior with the accuracy needed in clinical situations. Thus, test dependence as an exclusive way to assess suicidality should probably never be warranted. It appears reasonable to assume that psychological tests can identify those individuals who are similar to people of the same sex, age, and race that have committed suicide or that had made mild suicide attempts. Indeed, some tests have used this approach to varying degrees of success. However, it is not sufficient to know that someone may be at risk to take suicidal action. What is clinically essential is to determine the circumstances under which a person is vulnerable to resorting to suicidal behavior so the clinician can be forewarned and make appropriate interventions.

To gather the type of information needed to identify individuals at high risk and the potential precipitating circumstances, a broad battery of tests is needed to assess the spectrum of variables that have been found to be related to suicidal behavior such as demographics, personal and family history of suicide and suicide attempts, self-destructive ideation, attitude toward death, degree of hopelessness and pessimism about the future, and depression. In addition, this type of psychological assessment of suicide should include measures of long-standing characterological traits such as reality testing, judgment, action potential, and how the individuals view themselves and others (Eyman, Mikawa, & Eyman, 1990).

References

Beck, A. T., Kovacs, M., & Weissman, A. (1975). Hopelessness and suicidal behavior: An overview. *Journal of the American Medical Association, 234* (11), 1146–1149.

Beck, A. T., Kovacs, M., & Weissman, A. (1979). Assessment of suicidal intention: The Scale for Suicide Ideation. *Journal of Consulting and Clinical Psychology, 47,* 343–352.

Beck, R. W., Morris, J. B., & Beck, A. T. (1974). Cross-validation of the Suicidal Intent Scale. *Psychological Reports, 34,* 445–446.

Beck, A. T., Schuyler, D., & Herman, I. (1974). Development of suicidal intent scales. In A. T. Beck, H. L. P. Resnick, & D. J. Lettieri (Eds.), *The prediction of suicide* (pp. 45–56). Bowie, MD: Charles Press.

Beck, A. T., Steer, R. A., Kovacs, M., & Garrison, B. (1985). Hopelessness and eventual suicide: A 10-year prospective study of patients hospitalized with suicidal ideation. *American Journal of Psychiatry, 142*(5), 559–563.

Beck, A. T., Steer, R. A., & Ranieri, W. F. (1988). Scale for Suicide Ideation: Psychometric properties of a self-report version. *Journal of Clinical Psychology, 44*(4), 499–505.

Beck, A. T., Weissman, A., Lester, D., & Trexler, L. (1974). The measurement of pessimism: The Hopelessness Scale. *The Journal of Consulting and Clinical Psychology*, *42*(6), 861–865.

Beck, A. T., Weissman, A., Lester, D., & Trexler, L. (1976). Classification of suicidal behaviors, II: Dimensions of suicidal intent. *Archives of General Psychiatry, 33*, 835–837.

Braucht, G. N., & Wilson, L. T. (1970). Predictive utility of the revised Suicide Potential Scale. *Journal of Consulting and Clinical Psychology, 35*(3), 426.

Buglass, D., & McCulloch, J. W. (1970). Further suicidal behavior: The development and validation of predictive scales. *British Journal of Psychiatry, 116,* 483–491.

Chowdhury, N., Hicks, R., & Kreitman, N. (1973). Evaluation of an after-care service for parasuicide patients. *Social Psychiatry, 8,* 67–81.

Cull, J. G., & Gill, W. S. (1986). *Suicide Probability Scale (SPS): Manual.* Los Angeles, CA: Western Psychological Services.

Drake, R. E., Gates, C., & Cotton, P. G. (1986). Suicide among schizophrenics: A comparison of attempters and completed suicides. *British Journal of Psychiatry, 149,* 784–787.

Dyer, J. A. T., & Kreitman, N. (1984). Hopelessness, depression and suicidal intent in parasuicide. *British Journal of Psychiatry, 144,* 127–133.

Eyman, J. R., Mikawa, J. K., & Eyman, S. K. (In Preparation). The problem of adolescent suicide: Issues and assessments. In P. McReynolds & G. Chelune (Eds.), *Advances in psychological assessment: Vol. 7.*

Fawcett, J., Scheftner, W., Clark, D., Hedeker, D., Gibbons, R., & Coryell, W. (1987). Clinical predictors of suicide and patients with major affective disorders: A controlled prospective study. *American Journal of Psychiatry, 144*(1), 35–40.

Golding, S. L. (1985). Suicide Probability Scale. In J. W. Mitchell (Eds.), *Ninth mental measurements yearbook* (pp. 1500–1501). Lincoln, NE: University of Nebraska Press.

Goldney, R. D. (1979). Assessment of suicidal intent by a visual analog scale. *Australian and New Zealand Journal of Psychiatry, 13,* 153–155.

Holden, R. R., Mendonca, J. D., & Mazmanian, D. (1985). Relation of response set to observed suicide intent. *Canadian Journal of Behavioral Science, 17*(4), 359–368.

Inwald, R. E., Brobst, K. E., & Morrissey, R. F. (1987). *Hillson Adolescent Profile Manual.* Kew Gardens, NY: Hillson Research, Inc.

Johnson, J. H., & McCutcheon, S. (1981). Correlates of adolescent pessimism: A study of the Beck Hopelessness Scale. *Journal of Youth and Adolescence, 120*(2), 169–172.

Kazdin, A. E., French, N. H., Unis, A. S., Esveldt-Dawson, K., & Sherick, R. B. (1983). Hopelessness, depression, and suicidal intent among psychiatrically disturbed inpatient children. *Journal of Consulting and Clinical Psychology, 51-*(4), 504–510.

Kazdin, A. E., Rodgers, A., & Colbus, D. (1986). A hopelessness scale for children: Psychometric characteristics in concurrent validity. *Journal of Consulting and Clinical Psychology, 54*(2), 241–245.

Kovacs, M., Beck, A. T., & Weissman, A. (1975). Hopelessness: An indicator of suicidal risk. *Suicide, 5*(2), 98–103.

Lester, D., Beck, A. T., & Trexler, L. (1975). Extrapolation from attempted suicide to completed suicides. *Journal of Abnormal Psychology, 84*(5), 563–566.

McEvoy, T. L. (1974). Suicidal risk via the Thematic Apperception Test. In C. Neuringer (Ed.), *Psychological assessment of suicide risk* (pp. 95–117). Springfield, IL: Charles C Thomas.

Miller, I. W., Norman, W. H., Bishop, S. B., & Dow, M. G. (1986). The modified Scale for Suicidal Ideation: Reliability and validity. *Journal of Consulting and Clinical Psychology, 54*(5), 724–725.

Minkoff, K., Bergman, E., Beck, T.A., & Beck, R. (1973). Hopelessness, depression, and attempted suicide. *American Journal of Psychiatry, 130*(4), 455–459.

Miskimins, R. W., DeCook, R., Wilson, L. T., & Maley, R. F. (1967). Prediction of suicide in a psychiatric hospital. *Journal of Clinical Psychology, 23,* 296–301.

Miskimins, R. W., & Wilson, L. T. (1969). Revised Suicide Potential Scale. *Journal of Consulting and Clinical Psychology, 33*(2), 258.

Moore, J. T., Judd, L. L., Zung, W. W. K., & Alexander, G. R. (1979). Opiate addiction and suicidal behaviors. *American Journal of Psychiatry, 136*(9), 1187–1189.

Pallis, D. J. (1977). *The psychiatric assessment of attempted suicide: Personality, intent and suicide risk.* M.D. Thesis, University of Aberdeen. Pallis, D. J., Barraclough, B. M., Levey, A. B., Jenkins, J. S., & Sainsbury, P. (1982). Estimating suicide risk among attempted suicides: I. The development of new clinical scales. *British Journal of Psychiatry, 141,* 37–44.

Pallis, D. J., Gibbons, J. S., & Pierce, D. W. (1984). Estimating suicide risk among attempted suicides: II. Efficiency of predictive scales after the attempt. *British Journal of Psychiatry, 144,* 139–148.

Petrie, K., & Chamberlain, K. (1985). The predictive validity of the Zung Index of Potential Suicide. *Journal of Personality Assessment, 49,* 100–102.

Pierce, D. W. (1977). Suicidal intent in self-injury. *British Journal of Psychiatry, 130,* 377–385.

Resnick, J. H., & Kendra, J. M. (1973). Predictive value of the "Scale for Assessing Suicide Risk" (SASR) with hospitalized psychiatric patients. *Journal of Clinical Psychology, 29,* 187–190.

Silver, M. A., Bohnert, M., Beck, A. T., & Marcus, D. (1971). Relation of depression of attempted suicide and seriousness of intent. *Archives of General Psychiatry, 25,* 573–576.

Smith, K., Conroy, R. W., & Ehler, B. D. (1984). Lethality of suicide attempt rating scale. *Suicide and Life-Threatening Behavior, 14*(4), 215–242.

Smith, K., & Eyman, J. R. (April, 1986). Using the Lethality of Suicide Rating Scale to study the Suicide Intent Scale. Paper presented at the meeting of the American Association of Suicidology, Atlanta, GA.

Spirito, A. (1987). [Adolescent suicide attempters: SIQ Scores] unpublished data.

Topol, P., & Reznikoff, M. (1982). Perceived peer and family relationships, hopelessness and locus of control as factors in adolescent suicide attempts. *Suicide and Life-Threatening Behavior, 12*(3), 141–150.

Tuckman, J., & Youngman, W. F. (1968). A scale for assessing suicide risk of attempted suicides. *Journal of Clinical Psychology, 24,* 17–19.

Weissman, A. D., & Worden, J. W. (1974). Risk-rescue rating in suicide assessment. In A. T. Beck, H. L. P. Resnick, & A. J. Lettieri (Eds.), *The prediction of suicide* (192–213). Bowie, MD: Charles Press.

Wetzel, R. D. (1976). Hopelessness, depression, and suicide intent. *Archives of General Psychiatry, 33*(9), 1069–1073.

Wetzel, R. D., Margulies, T., Davis, R., & Karam, E. (1980). Hopelessness, depression, and suicide intent. *Journal of Clinical Psychiatry, 41*(5), 159–160.

Zung, W. W. K. (1971). A rating instrument for anxiety disorders. *Psychosomatics, 12,* (371–379).

Zung, W. W. K. (1974). Index of Potential Suicide (IPS): A rating scale for suicide prediction. In A. T. Beck, H.L.P. Resnick, & D.J. Lettieri (Eds.), *The prediction of suicide* (pp. 221–249). Bowie, MD: The Charles Press.

Zung, W. W. K., & Moore, J. (1976). Suicide potential in a normal adult population. *Psychosomatics, 27,* 37–41.

Chapter 3

THE YOUTH SUICIDE
RISK ASSESSMENT INTERVIEW

David A. Jobes, Ph.D. and Peter Cimbolic, Ph.D.

Introduction

There are few truisms in suicidology. However, one that is widely accepted is that effective intervention and treatment of a suicidal individual begins with a thorough risk assessment. When considering the range of instruments and methods used to evaluate suicide risk, perhaps the most valuable is the assessment interview. But as Curran (1987) has pointed out, the assessment and prediction of suicide is one of the most difficult challenges routinely facing even the most experienced mental health professional. Recent empirical findings suggest the average practicing psychologist has a better than 1 in 5 chance of losing a client to suicide during their career (Chemtob, Hamada, Bauer, Torigoe, & Kinney, 1988). Clearly, the stakes are high; yet, judging the likelihood of any potential suicide is very difficult. The weight of the challenge is intensified even further when the person being assessed is young.

Young people inherently bring to the counseling setting a unique set of developmental and emotional issues which complicate assessment. Young adulthood and adolescence is a time of tremendous change and turmoil. Adolescents are developmentally caught between childhood and adulthood, with the conflictual task of separating from the world of parents and family while simultaneously seeking protection from, and inclusion within, the family system (Berman, 1984). There is also a natural developmental distrust of adults inherent in youthful individuation/separation which can further complicate an assessment. An example of youthful distrust is seen when a young person tells a friend about their suicidal thoughts with the clear understanding that the peer is not to betray this confidence to an adult. Evidence of distrust of adults is suggested in the empirical literature. One recent study of completed youth suicides revealed that 83.3% had made suicidal threats in the week prior to their death, and, of these, half made their suicidal intention known *only* to a peer or sibling (Brent, Perper, Goldstein, Kolko, Allan, Allman, & Zelenak, 1988).

Other developmental forces also increase this assessment challenge. With limited life experience, youth tend to be more focused on the present rather than the future. When a young person experiences stress, there is a limited view of future possibilities—immediate solutions become more appealing (Berman, 1984). Adolescents have limited capacities to delay gratification. Simply, if something is wrong, it has to be fixed now. This is further complicated by the fact that suicidal fantasies are common in adolescence (Cantor, 1976). Adolescent impulsivity, limited problem-solving skills, and suicidal fantasies to escape pain can become lethal in combination. Further, as adolescents struggle to define themselves, they are highly vulnerable to peer influence and eager to imitate role models. This natural developmental inclination can provide a new source of concern in the form of a "suicide cluster" (see Chap. 7).

In summary, the unique forces of this age group provide a set of difficult obstacles to the already difficult task of assessing suicidal risk. While the challenges are considerable, an effective assessment interview of a potentially suicidal youth can be conducted with the assistance of the available empirical and clinical knowledge. The assessment interview can provide the critical starting point in treatment towards recovery, making a profound difference in a young life.

The Counseling Relationship

The fundamental value of the counseling relationship (and the techniques used to enhance it) cannot be overstated. A number of authors noted the importance of interpersonal contact between the therapist and the suicidal individual (Farberow, 1970; Hendin, 1981; Shneidman, 1980). Effective assessment and intervention often depends on how rapidly a supportive working relationship can be developed.

Hipple and Cimbolic (1979) feel the suicidal youth must know (and feel) they are talking to a person who is truly interested in their well-being. Any technique or approach that enhances the relationship and connectedness should be used. Eye contact, posture, and other nonverbal cues can be used to express a level of caring, interest, concern, and involvement. Empathic listening, mirroring of feelings, honesty, emotional availability, and warmth can help foster a sense of trust and create a willingness to examine possibilities other than self-destruction. While empathy and support are crucial, it is important to remember that suicidal adolescents often feel out of control. It is therefore sometimes necessary for the therapist to assume a more active and directive role than would normally be seen in therapy. A more "parental" role can be reassuring, bringing strength, steadiness, and structure to a time of crisis.

The Assessment Interview

The therapeutic relationship (alliance) is the primary vehicle of assessment and treatment, while empirical and clinical knowledge is used to assist in the interpretation of key variables which bear on the assessment of suicide risk. During the suicide assessment interview the therapist must listen closely, make direct inquiries, and assess/evaluate key variables and issues that we will describe throughout this chapter.

Cues to Suicide

The therapist must listen carefully for direct or indirect comments or nonverbal behaviors which may tip off suicidal thoughts and feelings. The majority of suicidal people provide a variety of clues to their self-destructive feelings. Close scrutiny of what the client says and how they behave is helpful in determining whether the potentially suicidal youth shares some commonality with those who have come before (Berman, 1988). Hipple and Cimbolic (1979) point out that suicidal individuals may make only veiled or disguised references to suicidal feelings. The therapist must be alert for veiled threats such as: "Sometimes I feel like just giving up"; "I'm just so tired, I just want to sleep"; "Things would be a lot better if I just weren't around." Indirect communications like giving up prized possessions, diary/journal entries, school essays, drawings, poems, or other artwork may reflect suicidal thoughts or feelings, as well.

Asking About Suicide

In suicide risk assessment, inquiries about suicidal thoughts and feelings should be direct. Vague suicidal comments should *always* elicit a direct question from the therapist as to whether the client is thinking about suicide (e.g. "Have you been thinking about killing yourself?"; "Sounds like you're feeling badly. Have you considered killing yourself?").

Further, Hipple and Cimbolic (1979) suggest that it is important to specifically determine the frequency and duration of suicidal thoughts and under what circumstances they occur.

Frankly, even for the experienced therapist, asking direct questions about suicide can be unsettling—there may be a tendency to underestimate the seriousness of the situation and a strong temptation to avoid directly asking about suicide. Some therapists fear that a direct inquiry might introduce a new and dangerous option which had not previously existed for the client (i.e. planting a seed for suicide).

While fear and avoidance are understandable, clinical and empirical evidence strongly support direct inquiry (Hipple & Cimbolic, 1979; Beck, Rush, Shaw, & Emory, 1979; Pope, 1986; Curran, 1987; Alberts, 1988; Berman, 1988). Direct inquiry is essential, in that it gives the potentially suicidal individual permission to discuss feelings that may have felt "undiscussable." Through direct inquiry the client can reveal their inner strugglings between life or death and openly discuss their feelings in a supportive, safe, and accepting climate. When a therapist is attentive to their suspicions of suicide, it has been our experience they will have been more often right than wrong (i.e. suicide will probably have been at least a consideration for the client). The dyad can easily move off the topic if suicide is genuinely not under consideration.

Psychological Intention

Many attempts have been made to operationally define the concept of suicide. Most define suicide as a death which is self-inflicted and psychologically intended (Jobes, Casey, Berman, & Wright, in press; Rosenberg et al., 1988). By definition, a victim who dies by a self-inflicted accidental death does not psychologically seek the end of their life, whereas one who dies by suicide does psychologically intend to die. For example, a death resulting from a self-inflicted gunshot wound would probably be considered an accident if the decedent was intoxicated and observed to be recklessly "horsing around" with a weapon that was thought to be unloaded. In contrast, another death resulting from a self-inflicted gunshot wound would probably be considered a suicide if the decedent was sober and observed to have methodically pointed and fired the weapon. In the latter case suicidal intent is directly inferred.

Clearly, the motive to end one's life versus seeking attention from a loved one are two very different kinds of desired outcomes and levels of intent. Berman (1988) has noted that the stated intent of a suicidal motive in young people is often interpersonal and instrumental. That is, the young person may turn to suicidal behavior as a means of exerting control over others by altering life circumstances, thereby punishing a loved one, seeking revenge, or communicating an otherwise unacceptable message. It therefore behooves the clinician to carefully evaluate the desired purpose, motive, and intent of the potential suicide act.

The Plan

The presence or absence of a suicide plan often reveals the desired consequences of the attempting behavior and provides one of the best indicators of intention and what may actually come to pass. Again, direct inquiry about a suicidal plan is necessary. If a plan is acknowledged, it is important to subsequently assess the lethality (or dangerousness) of the plan. The level of suicide intent can be directly inferred from certain features of the plan, particularly the potential lethality of the proposed method. Brent (1987) has empirically established that a robust relationship does indeed exist between medical lethality and suicide intent. Therefore, the planned use of more lethal methods (firearms, hanging, or jumping) reflects a greater degree of suicide intent in contrast to less lethal methods (overdoses or superficial cutting). In general, more lethal plans are those which are concrete and specifically include the use of highly dangerous methods. Similarly, the availability of (and knowledge about) lethal means heightens risk significantly. The risk of suicide is greatly increased, for example, if a suicidal youth has access to a firearm in the home and knows how to load and fire a gun.

During the assessment of the plan it may also be useful to evaluate how often the youth thinks of suicide. As described by Hipple and Cimbolic (1979), the situation-specificity and the extent/limits of the suicidal focus can be determined by establishing when and where thoughts of suicide occur, how long they last, and what leads to a discontinuation of such thoughts.

Rescuability and Reversability

A plan that minimizes the chance of intervention and rescue reflects a greater suicide risk. Conceptually and empirically, "potential for rescue" has been a central construct to two well-respected instruments which were specifically developed to assess the lethality of suicide attempts (see Weissman & Worden, 1974; Smith, Conroy, & Ehler, 1984). Simply, the less likely someone is able to intervene, the greater the risk.

Under the heading of rescue, both "reversability" of a chosen method
and "discoverability" of an attempt must be evaluated. A much higher
level of suicide intent and lethality can be inferred from an attempter
who plans to use an irreversible method (a gun) in contrast to a reversible
method (a drug overdose). The discoverability of a potential attempt
also reflects on the seriousness of suicide intent. A higher degree of
intent is clearly indicated by a plan to attempt suicide in a location with
little likelihood of intended or accidental discovery (e.g. an abandoned
warehouse, in the woods, etc.).

Suicide risk may be assessed as "low" in a case of a vague plan using a
few aspirin taken in front of a parent versus very "high" in a case where
an individual, experienced in the use of handguns and having access to a
gun, plans to go to a remote wooded area to shoot him/herself in the
head. However, it is also true that suicide deaths do occur in what would
appear to be highly reversible and discoverable situations; these are
sometimes referred to as accidental suicides. In one recent example, a
sixteen-year-old girl took an overdose at home using her father's heart
medication. Subsequently, the teenager told her parents and was immediately rushed to the hospital. Tragically, the youth cried that she did not
want to die and did not mean to hurt herself just prior to dying in her
mother's arms. Was this truly suicide? It was certainly death.

Suicide History

Another variable which bears significantly on suicide risk is the presence or absence of a suicidal history. Suicide risk increases significantly
when there is a history of *any* previous suicidality. It also increases in
relation to the extent of previous suicidal behaviors—current risk is less
serious if historically there has been only ideation, whereas the risk is
more serious if there were previous gestures and more serious still if
there were previous attempts. Similar to the assessment of plan, the more
concrete and specific the previous behavior, the greater the present
risk.

Beyond personal history of suicidality, family history of suicidal behavior and mood disorders have been linked to adolescent completions
(Shaffer, 1974; Shaffi, Carrigen, Whittinghill, & Derrick, 1985) and attempts
(Garfinkel, Froese, & Hood, 1982). As discussed by Brent et al. (1988), the
assessment of adult family members' psychiatric status with regard to
suicidal behavior and mood disorders may provide useful in the assessment of youth risk.

Assessing Youthful Pain

Through suicide the person often seeks to escape unendurable psychological pain (Shneidman, 1985). The pain which drives suicide must be understood idiosyncratically—what is painful to one person may not be to the next. Therefore, it is essential that the therapist be empathically aware of the youth's subjective experience of pain and its unique causes in *this* situation with *this* young person. However, as Curran (1987) has discussed, the youthful client may be unwilling or unable to communicate these painful feelings which presents a problem in risk assessment. This unwillingness to reveal suicidal thoughts can be severe enough to represent an emergency. It may then be necessary to confer with family and friends about the youth's recent emotional status. A best friend or teacher may be able to provide critical information concerning recent behaviors, changes in mood, and recent losses in the young person's life. However, when information is necessarily gained in this way, there is a chance that the ongoing therapeutic relationship could be damaged. Therefore, this is avoided if at all possible—particularly early in trying to establish an alliance with the youth.

While emotional pain is difficult at any age, young people can experience it especially intensely. The therapist must always respect the depth and degree of reported pain. Self-reports of extreme pain and trauma should not be discounted as adolescent melodrama. Their experience is acutely real and thereby potentially life-threatening. As discussed earlier, young people are present-oriented and lack life experience to provide the perspective needed to endure a painful period. It is important for the therapist to understand the youth's limited world view and life experience.

Given that risk increases as pain increases, it may be useful to have the young person actually rate their pain or hopelessness (e.g. ranging from "0" equaling absolutely no pain to "10" equaling absolutely unendurable pain). Subjective ratings can be helpful in increasing the therapist's understanding of the client's degree of pain. Additionally, subjective ratings can provide an ongoing barometer of suicide risk. Subsequent use of this "pain index" provides the opportunity to track changes over time in treatment.

Additional Risk Factors

A number of other risk variables have been empirically identified which are important to assess. This thirty-year body of research has illuminated a range of clinical, interpersonal, and psychopathological correlates of suicide risk.

CLINICAL CORRELATES. Beck and his colleagues (e.g. Kovacs, Beck, & Weissman, 1975; Beck, Brown, & Steer, 1989) suggest hopelessness may be the single best clinical indicator of suicide risk. Profound hopelessness and helplessness about oneself, others, and the future has been closely linked to depression and suicide (Rush & Beck, 1978; Beck, Brown, & Steer, 1989). A number of other correlates have also been identified (Berman, 1986; Brent et al., 1988, Shaffi et al., 1985). They include mood, particularly depressive, flat, or blunted affect; dramatic changes in affect; and isolation, stress, and emotional emptiness. There may also be free-floating rage, agitation, and fatigue. Often, a youth suicide attempt follows an emotionally laden precipitating event—a failure, a humiliation, or a rejection.

INTERPERSONAL VARIABLES. Young people can be very sensitive to societal and interpersonal pressures and the expectations of parents, siblings, peers, teachers, coaches, and girlfriends/boyfriends. Growing up in stressful families and having conflicted interpersonal relationships, the suicidal youth experiences blows to self-esteem, sense of self, and ability to cope (Berman, 1988). Research on the parents of suicidal youth has shown these parents have more overt conflicts and threats of separation or divorce, which result in the youth's experience of an early loss of a parent (Stanley & Barter, 1970; Corder, Shorr, & Corder, 1974; Miller, Chiles, & Barnes, 1982). Dykeman (1983) has noted that suicidal youth tend to feel alienated from the family unit.

Outside the family, there is evidence that suicidal youth have more frequent and serious problems with peers, are more sensitive, and are less likely to have a close confidant (McKenry, Tishler, & Kelly, 1982; Tishler & McKenry, 1982). A significant interpersonal loss such as a divorce of parents, death of a family member, or a romantic breakup may also trigger a suicidal crisis.

PSYCHOPATHOLOGY. Empirical research suggests that certain types of psychopathology tend to be correlated with suicidal behaviors. This is particularly true for mood disorders, especially manic-depressive illness or bipolar spectrum disorders (Garfinkel, Froese, & Hood, 1982; Robbins & Alessi, 1985; Brent et al., 1988). Unfortunately, however, suicide risk is not limited to mood disorders, in that increased rates of suicides and attempted suicide have also been linked to schizophrenia (McIntire, Angle, Wikoff, & Schlicht, 1977) and personality disorders—particularly borderline and antisocial disorders (Alessi, McManus, Brickman, & Grapentine, 1984; Berman, 1988). Also, alcohol and substance abuse is connected with youthful suicide behaviors (Brent et al., 1988; Tishler & McKenry, 1982). In suicidal situations alcohol/substance use can break down usual coping mechanisms and lead to decreased impulse control over self-destructive wishes. The therapist must be aware that young people with these disorders are at risk even though they might not verbalize suicidal intent. It follows that suicide potential should always be evaluated in cases when there is a history of an existing mental disorder.

Assessing Strengths and Weaknesses

During the assessment interview it is useful to evaluate the strength of negative pressures in the young person's life, counterbalanced against the positive influences. Various expectations and pressures can become overwhelming to the young person in the midst of a suicidal crisis, making effective action that much more difficult. A youth's ability to subjectively perceive skills and strengths may be lost in a time of crisis. As an example, an unacceptable performance such as an "F" grade on an exam could actually precipitate a suicide attempt for the heretofore outstanding student. Such a failure could represent the "end of the world" to an otherwise successful student who is determined to attend an Ivy League college.

Operationally, the therapist needs to directly ask a youth about their pressures or worries. They can ask the youth to place them into some kind of order to better evaluate their relative importance. Simultaneously, it is important to identify and assess the potential strengths, coping skills, and resources available. Reflecting back strengths and resources may provide some reassurance and perspective to the youth in crisis. The risk of suicide can be lessened when there is evidence of internal (e.g., cognitive) and external (e.g., interpersonal) resources for coping with conflict and stress (Berman, 1988).

Imminent Risk?

Ultimately, the assessment of suicide risk leads the therapist to consider a crucial question: Is the risk of self-harm behavior clear and imminent? The assessment of this question provides the basis for subsequent interventive strategies. Throughout the assessment of the variables previously described, the therapist must evaluate the degree and immediacy of the suicide risk for clinical, ethical, and legal purposes. While jurisdictionally dependent and differentially defined, law usually requires involuntary hospitalization (commitment) in cases where there is clear and imminent danger to self or others and voluntary hospitalization is refused (see Chapter 4 on treatment). The therapist must therefore establish whether the risk of suicide is acute and immediate or more chronic and long term. Is there sufficient agitation, upset, emotional energy, pressure, and pain to create an imminently dangerous situation requiring immediate interventive action on the part of the therapist?

As a precursor to intervention strategies described in the next chapter, it is important to note that most suicides (upwards of 80%) occur in an acute impulsive crisis; this is especially true for youthful populations. Only a small percentage of suicides within this group are methodically or rationally thought through. It can be reassuring to both the interventionist and the client that these crises are usually *transient.* Getting through the crisis phase provides the suicidal youth with the opportunity to consider more constructive and reversible options for coping.

Summary of Risk Assessment Interview

The effective assessment requires a genuine, empathic, honest, direct, and supportive therapeutic relationship and a thorough knowledge base about suicide risk factors, including demographic variables (see Chap. 1). When the relationship and knowledge are synthesized in an informed, sensitive, and thorough suicide assessment interview, the therapist is in a pivotal position to prevent or intervene in a premature and tragic death.

References

Alberts, F. L. (1988). Psychological assessment. In D. Capuzzi & L. Golden (Eds.), *Preventing adolescent suicide.* Muncie, Indiana: Accelerated Development Inc.
Alessi, N. E., McManus, M., Brickman, A., & Grapentine, L. (1984). Suicidal behav-

ior among serious juvenile offenders. *American Journal of Psychotherapy, 141,* 286–287.

Beck, A. T., Rush, A. J., Shaw, B. F., & Emery, G. (1979). *Cognitive therapy of depression.* New York: Guilford Press.

Beck, A. T., Brown, G., & Steer, R. A. (1989). Prediction of eventual suicide in psychiatric inpatients by clinical ratings of hopelessness. *Journal of Consulting and Clinical Psychology, 57,* 309–310.

Berman, A. L. (1984). The problem of teenage suicide. Testimony presented to the United States Senate Committee on the Judiciary Subcommittee on Juvenile Justice.

Berman, A. L. (1986). A critical look at our adolescence: Notes on turning 18 (and 75). *Suicide and Life-Threatening Behavior, 16,* 1–12.

Berman, A. L. (1988). Assessing the risk of suicidal behavior in adolescence. Invited article submitted to *Journal of Child and Adolescent Psychotherapy.*

Brent, D. A. (1987). Correlates of the medical lethality of suicide attempts in children and adolescents. *Journal of the American Academy of Child and Adolescent Psychiatry, 26,* 87–91.

Brent, D. A., Perper, J. A., Goldstein, C. E., Kolko, D. J., Allan, M. J., Allman, C. J., & Zelenak, J. P. (1988). Risk factors for adolescent suicide. *Archives of General Psychiatry, 45,* 581–588.

Cantor, P. (1976). Personality characteristics among youthful female suicide attempters. *Journal of Abnormal Psychology, 85,* 324–329.

Chemtob, C. M., Hamada, R. S., Bauer, G., Torigoe, R. Y., & Kinney, B. (1988). Patient suicide: Frequency and impact of psychologists. *Professional Psychology: Research and Practice, 19,* 833–845.

Comstock, B. (1979). Suicide in the 1970s: A second look. *Suicide and Life-Threatening Behavior, 9,* 3–13.

Corder, B. F., Shorr, W., & Corder, R. F. (1974). A study of social and psychological characteristics of adolescent suicide attempters in an urban, disadvantaged area. *Adolescence, 9,* 1–16.

Curran, D. K. (1987). *Adolescent suicidal behavior.* Washington: Hemisphere Publishing Corporation.

DeCatanzaro, D. (1981). *Suicide and Self-Damaging Behavior: A Sociobiological Perspective.* New York: Academic Press.

Durkheim, E. (1951). *Suicide: A study in sociology.* (J. S. Spaulding & G. Simpson, Trans., G. Simpson, Ed.). New York: Free Press. (Originally published, 1897).

Dykeman, B. F. (1983). Adolescent suicide: Recognition and intervention. *College Student Journal,* 364–368.

Farberow, N. (1970). The suicidal crisis in psychotherapy. In E. Shneidman, N. Farberow, & R. Litman (Eds.), *The psychology of suicide.* New York: Science House.

Garfinkel, B. D., Froese, A., & Hood, J. (1982). Suicide attempts in children and adolescents. *American Journal of Psychiatry, 139,* 1257–1261.

Hendin, H. (1981). Psychotherapy and suicide. *American Journal of Psychotherapy, 35,* 469–480.

Hipple, J., & Cimbolic, P. (1979). *The counselor and suicidal crisis.* Springfield, Illinois: Charles C Thomas.

Jobes, D. A., Berman, A. L., & Josselson, A. R. (1987). Improving the validity and reliability of medical-legal certifications of suicide. *Suicide and Life-Threatening Behavior, 17,* 310–325.

Kovacs, M., Beck, A. T., & Weissman, A. (1975). The use of suicidal motives in the psychotherapy of attempted suicides. *American Journal of Psychotherapy, 29,* 363–368.

McIntire, M. S., Angle, C. R., Wikoff, R. L., & Schlicht, M. L. (1977). Recurrent adolescent suicidal behavior. *Pediatrics, 60,* 605–608.

McKenry, D., Tishler, C., & Kelley, C. (1982). Adolescent suicide: A comparison of attempters and non-attempters in an emergency room population. *Clinical Pediatrics, 21,* 266–270.

Miller, M. L., Chiles, J. A., & Barnes, V. E. (1982). Suicide attempters within a delinquent population. *Journal of Consulting and Clinical Psychology, 50,* 491–498.

Murray, H. A. (1938). *Explorations in personality.* New York: Oxford University Press.

Pope, K. S. (1986). Assessment and management of suicidal risk: Clinical and legal standards of care. *The Independent Practitioner, 6,* 17–23.

Richman, J. (1986). *Family therapy for suicidal people.* New York: Springer.

Robbins, D., & Alessi, N. (1985). Depressive symptoms and suicidal behavior in adolescents. *American Journal of Psychiatry, 142,* 588–592.

Rosenberg, M. L., Davidson, L. E., Smith, J. C., Berman, A. L., Buzbee, H., Gantner, G., Gay, G., Moore-Lewis, B., Mills, D. H., Murray, D., O'Carroll, P. W., & Jobes, D. A. (1988). Operational criteria for the determination of suicide. *Journal of Forensic Sciences, 32,* 1445–1455.

Rush, A. J., & Beck, A. T. (1978). Cognitive therapy of depression and suicide. *American Journal of Psychotherapy, 32,* 201–219.

Shaffer, D. (1974). Suicide in childhood and early adolescence. *Journal of Child Psychology and Psychiatry, 15,* 275–291.

Shafii, M., Carrigen, S., Whittinghill, J. R., & Derrick, A. (1985). Psychological autopsy of completed suicide in children and adolescents. *American Journal of Psychiatry, 142,* 1061–1064.

Shneidman, E. S. (1980). Psychotherapy with suicidal patients. In T. B. Karasu & L. Bellak (Eds.), *Specialized techniques in individual psychotherapy.* New York: Brunner/Mazel.

Shneidman, E. S. (1985). *Definition of suicide.* New York: John Wiley & Sons, Inc.

Shneidman, E. S. (1988). Some reflections of a founder. *Suicide and Life-Threatening Behavior, 18,* 1–12.

Shneidman, E. S. (1989). Conversation hour: Conversation with Dr. Edwin Shneidman. Presentation at the 22nd annual conference of the American Association of Suicidology, San Diego, California.

Smith, K., Conroy, R. W., & Ehler, B. D. (1984). Lethality of suicide attempt rating scale. *Suicide and Life-Threatening Behavior, 14,* 215–242.

Stanley, E. J., & Barter, J. J. (1970). Adolescent suicidal behavior. *American Journal of Orthopsychiatry, 40,* 87–96.

Tishler, C., & McKenry, P. (1982). Parental negative self and adolescent suicide attempters. *Journal of the American Academy of Child Psychiatry, 21,* 404–408.

Weissman, A., & Worden, W. (1972). Risk-rescue rating in suicide assessment. *Archives of General Psychiatry, 26,* 553–560.

Chapter 4

TREATMENT OF SUICIDAL YOUTH

Peter Cimbolic, Ph.D. and David A. Jobes, Ph.D.

Introduction

The treatment of a suicidal youth involves two phases of interventions aimed first at diffusing the danger of the acute crisis and then addressing the underlying developmental issues which led to the suicidal vulnerability. As discussed earlier, treatment is closely linked to ongoing assessment of suicide risk. The continuous and dynamic synthesis of assessment and treatment is the essence of the effective management and eventual resolution of the youth's suicidal crisis. While a wide range of treatment alternatives are available, our focus will be on skill building, particularly problem solving, and how these skills relate to improving self-esteem. There will also be an examination of the unique ethical and legal considerations inherent in working with suicidal clients in general and youthful clients in particular. While the prospects of working with a suicidal youth can be simultaneously challenging and fear-inducing, the clinician has a wide range of treatment alternatives and strategies which can facilitate the process by which death becomes a non-viable option in the face of living alternatives.

Before turning to our two-phase treatment of suicidal youth, two a priori considerations are important to keep in mind. First, suicidal feelings, thoughts, and behaviors are all symptoms which are not unique to any one particular diagnostic category or problem type—each suicidal youth must be understood individually and idiosyncratically. A second, and somewhat paradoxical, consideration is that suicidal youth do share many of the same psychological, dynamic, diagnostic, familial, social, and personal variables—many suicidal young people have similar psychological and behavioral profiles, which allows for conceptual clarity. Therefore, the treatment plan must take into account both the unique characteristics of the suicidal youth while understanding and using the knowledge base which broadly applies to suicidal youth.

The Two-Phase Treatment of Suicidal Youth

Case example: A sixteen-year-old boy becomes suicidal following what he perceives as a series of causal precipitating events—school failure, parental conflict, broken romantic relationships. In terms of treatment, the immediate focus has to be the client's safety and reactions to the "triggering events." For safety to be insured, the client must see that there are other ways of dealing with these events more effectively than through suicide. Therefore, simultaneous and concrete steps must be taken to both ensure physical safety while parallel problem-solving and coping strategies are examined. Towards this goal, the clinician may choose to establish a contract insuring physical safety with the youth, collect the stash of pills, and involve the parents in treatment to help de-escalate the dangerousness of the crisis situation.

After the acute phase of the suicidal crisis is resolved, the clinician's focus shifts to the second phase of treatment which deals with the underlying dynamics, historical issues, and developmental issues which were at the roots of the vulnerabilities which eventually led to the suicidal crisis. The clinician in the previous example may have chosen to explore the youth's conflicts with parents, fears of failure, or feelings of rejection. Thus, a two-phased treatment approach allows the resolution of the immediate crisis but does not ignore the more pervasive underlying developmental themes.

Phase I—Crisis Intervention

Crisis intervention, by definition, requires the employment of clinical skills and behaviors that may not be normally used in ongoing psychotherapy. During the acute crisis phase of treatment, the clinician must necessarily be much more active and take much more responsibility for, and try to take control of, the welfare of the acutely distressed youth. This active "take-charge" role is a sharp contrast to the more passive traditional position taken by therapists which normally encourages clients to confront and assume responsibility for their own lives. However, in the crisis situation the clinician must become "powerful" in the presence of the client's powerlessness.

A central goal in this phase of treatment is to develop a strong trusting alliance between the client and the clinician. In our opinion, therapist availability during the crisis is an essential ingredient in forging this alliance. Unfortunately, it is all too common for suicidal ideation and impulses to be present and disturbing to the suicidal youth outside the scheduled therapeutic hour. In working with a youth in crisis the therapist must attempt to be available during times of need and the client should be instructed to call and talk about their dangerous thoughts or feelings during these times of acute distress outside the therapy hour. As Shrier (1987) suggests,

> It is at these times of crisis that the therapist must often endure periods of being tested, even used and manipulated. Not surprisingly, many of these suicidal clients provoke and then anticipate rejection. They feel very lonely and isolated, even when they appear to be surrounded by friends. The fear of becoming attached to another because of the risk of another painful loss. (P. 341.)

These dynamics place the clinician in a difficult "therapeutic" predicament—trying to establish essential trust with a distrustful youth. The therapist must be able to tolerate being put through the youth's emotional wringer to eventually earn this trust.

Simultaneously, the clinician needs to establish a firm understanding or "contract" with the client that they will not hurt themselves, what Hipple and Cimbolic (1979) have referred to as a "no-kill contract." Such a contract, verbal or written, represents a working understanding between the client and the therapist that the client will not harm him/herself for a mutually agreed upon period of time in order to allow treatment to proceed without hospitalization. Of course, the longer the period of time to which the therapist can get the client to agree, the better. Similarly, the more concrete the contract, the better. A written contract with specific provisions, even a contingency plan, is always stronger than a verbal contract.

An example typical of a no-kill contract agreement would include: (a) a clear promise from the client to not hurt or kill themselves for an allotted period of time (e.g. the next 2 days, weeks, months, or until the next appointment at which time the contract can be renegotiated); and (b) a contingency plan of what the client is to do if they feel acutely suicidal (e.g. a series of commitments to call the therapist, a friend, a family member, or a crisis hot line). It is important to note that since the client is agreeing not to hurt themselves, the clinician must be able to give the client the reassurance of availability and backup resources. In effect, the therapist must use him/herself and the therapeutic relationship as "bargaining chips" to preserve the client's safety.

Central to the specifics of contracting and management of an acute case is the ongoing attempt to negotiate for longer and longer periods of time in the no-kill contracts. Suicide has often been described as the permanent solution for a temporary problem. Simply stated, the clinician must obtain time from the youthful client to be able to work out a more satisfactory solution than suicide. Initially, it may be necessary for the therapist to emphasize that it is indeed the *therapist* who needs more time to help the youth to identify more effective coping strategies.

Hopelessness is a universal feeling found in virtually all suicidal individuals including youth (Beck et al., 1989). Acutely suicidal individuals both think and feel that no matter what they do, it will not make any difference to take the pain away. All they can see and feel is pain and despair. The cognitive distortions and affective paralysis inherent in the acute suicidal state demand that the therapist be the personification of hope (if just for now). The clinician can empathically validate and legitimize that the client does not feel hope at this time, seeing no light at the end of the tunnel. By empathically understanding the client's hopeless perspective, the therapist is in a better position to negotiate and extract a promise that the client will not hurt themselves for the agreed-upon period of time (again, the longer the better). Once this understanding is established, both the client and the clinician have created therapeutic breathing room so that therapeutic progress can be made beyond mere crisis management.

Once the therapist has negotiated the no-kill contract, an additional (and frequently ignored) step is needed. The clinician must ensure that the availability of the intended means of attempt is literally removed from ready accessibility to the prospective victim. In the case of a potential overdose, the clinician may request that the client bring their stash of pills to the therapist. If a gun was to be used, the clinician may request that parents remove firearms from the home environment or store such weapons in a safe place from the youth, particularly as firearms now account for almost two of every three adolescent suicidal deaths in the United States (Berman, 1987). Clinicians have to become explicitly involved in insuring that the planned means of suicide is removed to whatever extent possible. No single act can decrease the dangerousness (lethality) of the crisis situation more than removing the means. Further, the actual act of turning over the intended self-destructive means may have a tremendous symbolic value. The client can benefit from the experience of turning over the means of death to the person who is temporarily serving as the vehicle for life. It may also help resolve the anguishing painful ambivalence around the decision as to whether to attempt suicide, with the result being that the client finally feels safe and protected.

FUNCTIONAL/INSTRUMENTAL MOTIVES. Berman (1987) suggests that suicidal behaviors have functional or "instrumental" motives (i.e. these behaviors may consciously or unconsciously serve to meet various purposes or needs). Sometimes the motive(s) for suicide is not even completely understood by the potential attempter. At a more primitive level, every serious suicide ideator simply wants the pain to end. They feel pessimistic about the future and their ability to deal with it. However, suicidal motivations are seldom this straightforward; more often, they involve complex intrapsychic and interpersonal components.

One technique which may be particularly helpful in trying to untangle this web of complex motives involves asking the young person to identify what they would like each survivor to understand or know as a function of their future suicide if it had been completed. As strange as it may sound, suicide is a form of communication, albeit imprecise and with no opportunity for reclarification. This simple inquiry often helps facilitate the youth's ability to identify thoughts and feelings related to each significant other in their life and messages they may wish to communicate to them through their suicidal behavior.

For some youths these feelings can be very raw and primitive, while for others the feelings may be more complex and elaborate. Examples of typical responses to the communication inquiry vary widely. To a mother or father the message might be, " . . . for them to understand how much I hate them" or " . . . just to show them." To a boyfriend or girlfriend the message might be, " . . . to show them how much I love them" or " . . . that I can't live without them." By helping the client verbalize these thoughts and wishes it may help the youth come to a richer understanding of the symbolic value s/he is hoping others will attach to their demise. Once these intended communications become clarified, the youth may be gently confronted with the reality that there are no guarantees of how others will feel or think following the suicide. The obvious goal then is to help the youth communicate these thoughts and feelings more directly.

PSYCHOPATHOLOGY. During this acute phase of crisis intervention, more traditional diagnostic considerations may be of some importance. As indicated earlier, suicidal ideation is a symptom and not unique to any particular form of psychopathology. Further, suicidal thoughts and behavior may occur among individuals who do not fit into any diagnos-

tic category. Suicidal thoughts or feelings may be the primary or only
identifiable diagnostic consideration. Suicidal ideation, however, may
also occur in the presence of psychopathology and be a function or
consequence of a particular type of psychopathology. In general, during
the crisis management phase of treatment, the presence of suicidal impulses
or threats have to be taken into consideration in the overall treatment
plan. But the primary treatment focus normally will be the containment
of the acute psychopathology—facilitating both behavioral and emotional control as quickly as possible. For example, during those occa-
sions where there is an active psychotic process the risk of suicidal
behavior increases significantly. In such situations the clear treatment
focus for suicide centers on bringing the psychotic process under control,
with the understanding that once the psychotic process is no longer
present the associated suicidal impulses will also probably remit.

The three most frequently encountered psychotic conditions seen in
emergency rooms and inpatient psychiatric facilities that may have accom-
panying suicidal risk are: (a) bipolar disorder, manic phase; (b) brief
reactive psychosis emerging into a schizophrenic disorder; and (c) drug-
induced psychotic states from any number of offending agents including
but not limited to PCP, amphetamines, and hallucinogens.

The treatment decisions in each of these situations will be driven in
part by the clinician's understanding of the client's diagnosis. However,
one treatment goal independent of diagnosis is to provide a safe, non-
threatening refuge and to stabilize the client enabling them to gain
behavioral control as soon as possible. Medications are usually withheld
if at all possible for a number of reasons. In the event the psychotic state
was drug induced, the introduction of another drug can cause a possible
potentially dangerous drug interaction. However, drugs are also withheld to diagnostically determine if environmental interventions alone,
or in combination with support, can lead to the gradual resolution of the
acute psychotic state. Another consideration is that the long-term or
ongoing use of drugs during the balance of treatment is not preferable,
since young people do not tolerate drugs or their side effects well. Young
clients are often highly treatment resistant to medications in their desire
to not be controlled by them which is understandable given their feelings of distrust.

Medications, however, are indicated when safe treatment is unable to
proceed without them. In these situations, the drugs chosen will depend
upon the type of symptoms present and the type of psychopathology.

There is no specific drug for treating suicidal ideation or behavior; drug choice is symptomatically and diagnostically specific. For example, a likely drug choice for someone with symptoms of a bipolar mood disorder, manic episode, would be lithium carbonate. However, it is important to note that lithium carbonate takes 5–14 days to exert "antimanic" effects. In the meantime the clinician may be faced with a young person who remains behaviorally out of control, in which case it may be necessary to use an antipsychotic/neuroleptic until the lithium "kicks in." Use of these latter types of medications will often permit behavioral containment within 24–48 hours. Neuroleptics are generally avoided if at all possible, since they have side effects that are not tolerated well, particularly in youthful populations. Young people are in fact more at risk to developing certain types of these side effects (e.g. acute dystonic reactions).

Schizophreniform disorders which often include frightening delusions and hallucinations present difficult treatment choices. Again, drugs are probably going to be withheld if at all possible. In those cases where use of medication cannot be withheld, the neuroleptics/antipsychotics will often be employed. In general, if the clinician is faced with a youth experiencing their first psychotic episode (particularly if their pre-episode history has been socially and academically unremarkable), the neuroleptic discontinuance should occur as soon as clinically possible, since the long-term problems related to use of these medications can result in permanent neurological and behavioral changes.

The best treatment for drug-induced psychotic states caused by street drugs is usually time and support while safety from erratic and self-destructive behaviors is insured. In this type of crisis it is important for the clinician to be able to observe how the individual changes over time symptomatically, psychologically, and behaviorally as the offending drug is metabolized in the body. The clinician may miss this opportunity if (and when) additional drugs are introduced into the formula. A hospital setting permits a "wait-and-see" treatment stance for a drug-induced psychosis and is the most prudent treatment strategy.

Suicidal behavior and ideation is also seen in profound depressions that may be at least partly biologically determined. Evidence that would support such a biological hypothesis would be a strong family history of serious depression (e.g. major depressive episodes, particularly when there has been a clear family history of positive treatment responses to antidepressant medications). Antidepressant medication can be particularly useful in treating this limited subset of depressions. But once again, the nature of the symptoms, the family and personal history, would be the evidence for antidepressant use—not the presence of suicidal behavioral/ideation.

One important consideration from the suicide interventionist's perspective is that antidepressant medications take a long time to work. The antidepressant effects of any of these drugs take from a minimum of 2–3 weeks to as much as 2–3 months before maximum clinical effects may be observed. Further complicating the antidepressant option is that they are all extremely toxic in overdose (with two exceptions). Therefore, the very drugs used to treat depression and related suicidality may be used as a lethal method of attempting suicide, and tragically have been.

TREATMENT SETTING. In the crisis phase, an important early treatment consideration confronting the clinician is the determination of an appropriate treatment setting. The choice of treatment setting depends on a number of considerations, mostly clinical, although legal and economic factors may also come into play. The setting choice basically involves a decision to either treat the youth on an inpatient or outpatient basis. Determination of treatment setting is relatively straightforward following the occurrence of a serious suicide attempt. However, even after serious attempts, the choice of setting or treatment to be employed is not always obvious.

The first place a suicide attempt is discovered is often in the emergency room of the local hospital. While emergency room personnel may be competent to handle the medical aspects of the emergency, they may not be trained or sensitive to the psychiatric/psychological aspects of a suicidal emergency. This may result in the psychological aspects of the suicidal crisis being largely ignored or undertreated. Increasingly, in recognition of this latter reality, efforts have been undertaken to sensitize emergency room personnel to be more aware and vigilant of the psychological aspects of suicidal emergencies. As Corder and Haizlip (1982) note, the family physician and pediatric emergency room personnel are the most frequent initial contacts with suicidal children and are therefore in a unique position to determine the eventual care a suicidal youth should receive. Based on this data, substantial efforts have been undertaken to educate and sensitize nursing and physician emergency room personnel to psychological aspects of suicidal emergencies (Keidel, 1983; Litt et al., 1983).

Unfortunately, client and familial denial may also first become evident in the emergency room setting. Recommendations for continued hospitalization (by way of admission into the hospital following emergency room treatment) are very frequently ignored by suicide attempters and their families. As Litt et al. (1983) have discussed, only one-third of suicide attempters who are treated for the medical aspects of their attempt follow subsequent treatment recommendations to receive follow-up mental health care. This finding has led these authors to conclude that hospital administrators and professionals should reconsider their inpatient admission guidelines following suicide attempts. Specifically, they suggest that even in the context of a "mild" attempt from a medical perspective, more routine hospital admissions are perhaps warranted.

It is well established in the literature that one of the best predictors of eventual suicide completion is number of previous attempts. Simply stated, the greater the number of attempts, the greater the likelihood of eventual suicide. The preceding is relevant to a discouraging finding of the Litt et al. (1983) study. These authors found in the sample that essentially all first attempters complied with recommendations for follow-up care, whereas 60% of multiple attempters (at least one previous attempt) were non-compliant with follow-up care recommendations. These findings suggest that those who are most likely to be treatment refusing may be the very patients most at risk for eventual completion of suicide.

Hospitalization presents a number of advantages in treating youth who are seriously at risk for suicidal behavior. Most obviously, admission to an inpatient setting literally removes the young person from the stressors and the environment which may have contributed to the suicidal crisis. Hospitalization also clearly communicates to the potential victim that their emotional status and risk of suicide is being seriously perceived and treated. The stark reality of being hospitalized may also serve to break down familial denial. Hospitalization also brings control to a situation that up until then had been out of control. As Shrier (1987) notes: "Hospitalization offers immediate relief from the pressures that precipitated the suicide attempt or gesture and may relieve anxiety and provide a supportive, protective, and caring setting" (p. 342).

From the clinician's perspective, hospitalization permits the simultaneous participation of multiple providers, thereby diluting the understandable negative countertransference that often emerges during the treatment of suicidal adolescents and young adults. The diffusion of treatment responsibility inherent in hospital settings permits the "spreading" of responsibilities for care to an entire system and not just to a single person or clinician during the crisis phase of care. The inpatient treatment system provides resources which can be activated as needed—24 hours a day, seven days a week.

There are numerous types of hospital facilities and programs available for treating a suicidal youth. These settings may range from general inpatient psychiatric wards in community-based hospitals to unlocked wards (with pediatricians, clinical social workers, psychologists, and nurse counselors) designed specifically for the adolescent (Greydanus et al., 1986; Piersma & Van Wingen, 1988).

The clinical decision to hospitalize is a "case-management" decision. Can the crisis situation be resolved and the client be treated safely in their environment, or is it too dangerous to allow the client to remain in their environment? The clinician may come to the judgment that in the interest of the youth's safety a hospital would be the most appropriate setting. This recommendation can then be made to the youth and his/her family, which they may or may not accept. However, if the level of suicidal risk is of "clear and imminent danger," then, independent of family or client wishes, the clinician must be the instrument of involuntary hospitalization or commitment. Involuntary hospitalization is generally the exception rather than the rule, but in these exceptional cases the therapist must be prepared to act even though such seemingly high-handed behaviors are often difficult to accept. Simply stated, clinicians are not accustomed to being in the position of having to *make* clients do anything, especially something against the client's will.

When there is less client and family resistance, the possibility of hospitalization can be approached more rationally and matter-of-factly as to why it may be appropriate at this time. Hospitalization can be simply presented as a necessary treatment alternative for specific reasons over a discrete period of time. Contrary to the adversarial stance described above, the client and family may take great relief and comfort that somebody else is willing to take care of the suicidal youth; the respective parties may feel they have reached their limits in their ability to cope with the situation and are relieved to let go of the feelings of responsibility.

The hospitalization of the youth can be framed as a genuine opportunity for the youth and the family system to address and intervene in individual and family dysfunction (Shrier, 1987; Walker & Mehr, 1983). Walker and Mehr suggest that hospitalization resulting from serious suicide ideation or attempt can throw the family into a state of "disequilibrium." Hospitalization legitimizes this disequilibrium and provides the therapist an opportunity to translate the adolescent's cry for

help within the family system such that it can be heard and understood
for what it really is: a desperate message of hopelessness and pain. Thus,
hospitalization may serve to convert "a potentially fatal act into a constructive and viable growth experience for the adolescent and all family
members" (Walker & Mehr, 1983, p. 285).

The hospital provides a safe and "neutral" setting in which family
dynamics (to whatever extent they are contributing to the crisis) can be
explored. Some suicidal motives can best be understood as being symp-
tomatic of more pervasive familial dysfunction, not just the individual
issues of the youth. This is particularly more likely to be the case for the
younger youth. The younger adolescent is much more likely to "blame"
his or her distress on forces that occur within the family system, while
the older adolescent or young adult who is suicidal is more likely to
attribute their suicidal ideation to factors outside the family system
(although family issues may be one of the factors within the constellation
of many factors).

Phase II—Treatment Resolution

The crisis intervention phase of intervention lasts as long as there is a
crisis. This phase of treatment is usually of brief duration, generally
lasting two weeks to a month, although it may feel like an eternity for the
treatment provider. Once the clinician and client have forged a strong
working alliance—characterized by trust and reassurances on the part of
the youth that suicide is no longer under consideration—the stage is set
for a careful examination of the personal, situational, familial, social,
and academic/work forces that allowed suicidal vulnerability to emerge.
It is essential that suicide assessment and intervention does not stop
when the acute crisis subsides. Premature termination of treatment is
discouraged, particularly given the therapeutic dyad has worked to
achieve the unique position of having survived the suicidal crisis. Having done this, there exists an intact therapeutic relationship with a
demonstrated capacity to be healing. While the crisis may be over,
underlying developmental themes remain that will continue to be problematic if left untreated and may even lead to subsequent suicidal episodes.
However, through ongoing care these issues, problems, and themes that
led to suicidal vulnerability can be addressed in the resolution phase of
the therapy process. Not all suicidal youths have difficulty with the same
underlying themes; rather, each young person will tend to have their
own unique set of issues which will repeat themselves if left untreated.

A number of treatment approaches which have been described in the literature are appropriate during the phase of treatment resolution. These treatment modalities range from traditional longer-term individual therapy (Hendin, 1981; Toolin, 1962), to shorter-term individual treatment (Beck & Beck, 1978; Getz, Allen, Myers, & Linder, 1983), to group treatment (Comstock & McDermott, 1975; Farberow, 1976; Hipple, 1982). For youthful populations family therapy may be particularly effective (Alanen, Rinne, Paukkonen, 1981; Richman, 1979, 1986). However, there is no persuasive empirical evidence that one particular school of therapy or treatment approach is clearly superior to the others in therapeutic outcomes.

Given this, most clinicians develop their own eclectic blend of treatment approaches in dealing with the youthful suicidal client. While a detailed discussion of each approach is beyond the scope of the present discussion, the following approach can be readily integrated into any of the other modalities.

TREATMENT THROUGH PROBLEM SOLVING. In general, emotionally disturbed adolescents have been found to be poor problem solvers (Platt, Spivack, Altman, Altman, & Peizer, 1974). Additional empirical findings have indicated that suicidal youth are particularly deficient in problem-solving skills (Hynes, 1976; Levenson & Neuringer, 1971). Recent work has further demonstrated that unipolar depressions can be effectively treated by problem-solving strategies (Nezu, 1986; Nezu & Perri, 1989). Poor problem-solving skills/abilities coupled with poor self-esteem are two interrelated and intertwined themes which are commonly seen in suicidal youth. In general, suicidal youth can clearly identify what is wrong in their lives. These young people often know a lot about the causes of their pain but remain convinced that there is nothing which can help. As Frederick (1985) notes, most suicidal youth can be described by their marked feelings of haplessness, hopelessness, and helplessness. Such feelings can be readily related to poor problem-solving skills. Therefore, a straightforward problem-solving treatment approach can be a very useful means to address central emotional and cognitive issues and related deficits and how these may have led to poor self-esteem.

Suicidal youth experience haplessness as having had more than their share of bad breaks or bad luck. Hopelessness is experienced as the inability to see how things could possibly be better. This hopelessness blocks the youth from experiencing whatever positive forces are present in their life. "Helplessness" cause the youth to believe that whatever they do will have no effect or won't make any difference. Outcomes are not perceived as being related to their behaviors. Such feelings destroy any sense of self-efficacy, resulting in impoverished self-esteem.

In order to help the client identify problem-solving and decision-making deficits, the therapist invites the client to examine the major problem areas in life, having them look at choices made at various choice points related to each identified problem. This process can be helpful in allowing the client to realize that there were a range of decision-making alternatives at each choice point for each problem, some of which may have not resulted in failed outcome. Similarly, the therapist can help the client look at the present problem areas in their lives—and help them examine existing decision-making alternatives. The client and therapist can then try to anticipate what outcomes/consequences would or could result as a function of any given action step or problem-solving strategy if it were to be implemented.

An ongoing problem-solving therapy approach can serve a number of purposes. First, it directly confronts the themes of haplessness, helplessness, and hopelessness. It also allows the client to come to accept responsibility for their behaviors and their outcomes. In the course of this process, the client hopefully begins to realize that other strategies or action steps may have not led to negative outcomes. Ultimately, the client can come to understand that they themselves had a major role in their "bad luck." Therein, the client may come to accept that they were not a victim but were largely responsible for what happened in their lives.

But, the purpose of this process is not to have the client place blame on themselves for past problem-solving failures. Rather, the goal is to have them see that there were alternative solutions to the ones they employed, and these may have had different outcomes. As stated in the previous chapter, young people have very limited life experiences and not a wealth of problem-solving histories in comparison to adults. They also usually do not have the opportunity to think out and speak about their internal decision-making process in the presence of a more mature, experienced, non-judgmental decision maker—the therapist.

Having the young person actively weigh decision-making alternatives during the therapy process allows the young adult a chance to develop better decision-making skills, thus having them feel empowered in the face of their heretofore feelings of helplessness. During this process, the clinician does not sit in judgment as to which decision is the "best" decision within a range of choices. Rather, in this kind of therapy, the clinician helps the young person weigh relative strengths and weaknesses of each decision-making alternative.

Another parallel strategy during this process is for the therapeutic dyad to actively evaluate the adequacy of the data upon which client decisions are being made. Here, too, the young person can be victimized by their limited life experiences and make decisions that are based on inadequate, poor, or insufficient data. It can be said that people never make a wrong decision. Every decision ever made is the best decision given the available data at the time the decision is made. As time passes and new data emerges, then, and only then, can one evaluate whether this new data supports what had been decided or flies in the face of the previously rendered decision. Thereby, each person is able to judge any given decision only over time and with the luxury of hindsight.

Therefore, it is sometimes necessary to confront the client about the timing of a potential decision. Is this a decision that can wait until more or better data is available? Delaying a decision may be frustrating for the young person given the urgency they bring to most things, including decision making. The timing of a decision should be subject to close scrutiny within the therapy process. If the client comes to the conclusion that more data may be available and if the decision can be delayed until that data is gathered, the therapist and client can explore where and how the new data may be obtained.

If, however, through the therapeutic process the client arrives at the conclusion that a decision has to be made at this time with the data at hand, the clinician can "devil's advocate" every decision-making choice available to the client. This permits the client to see there is not just one choice. Any choice will have potential merits and potential pitfalls.

Clearly, if this kind of active decision-making work is applied across multiple decisions confronting the client over an extended period of time during therapy, the client has the opportunity to develop more mature and hopefully more effective decision-making skills and strategies which can be used outside therapy. This process permits the client's sense of helplessness to be challenged and subsequently resolved. The acquisition of active decision-making skills can provide for the youth new feelings of mastery, competence, and confidence, taking the place of helplessness, haplessness, and hopelessness. In time, the client is able to "own" the changes and internalize them into their self-system, thereby increasing self-esteem.

It is also important for both therapist and client to monitor and, if possible, identify where there is improvement and how it has taken place. It may be useful to have the client discuss their change process— how are things different today than yesterday? What are they doing differently today than yesterday and what are the differences in outcomes? By continuously asking the client to verbally display these comparative differences, the client is better able to understand and internalize how they are changing and how these changes affect their feelings about themselves.

One way to facilitate this "owning" of changes in self-esteem can be by the use of "person-in-the-mirror" technique. This technique can be useful in initially assessing baseline self-esteem but may also helpful in assessing subtle changes as they occur over time in therapy. To use this technique, the clinician merely asks the client how they feel about the person in the mirror—meaning the client. This provides a structure and metaphor through which the client can carefully introspect feelings about themselves, their various characteristics and traits.

Too often, young clients get caught up in being externally focused— they are hyper-vigilant in their attempts to assess what others think of them. They can quickly describe both negative and sometimes positive feedback they have received from significant others in their lives. However, getting the client to shift the focus internally away from the external can be difficult, particularly where peer pressure for conformity is enormous. The assessment of the client's feelings about the person in the mirror provides a lens of evaluation for the client while providing insight about the client's self-system to the therapist.

This technique provides a window to the client's feelings about themselves—good, bad, strengths, weaknesses—all from the client's perspective. It provides a means of focusing so that clients can define and articulate those parts of themselves that they do not like. It can further enhance the therapeutic alliance, since it is the *client* who is identifying the focus of treatment—not an authority figure telling the youth what is "wrong" with them. Weekly inquiry about feelings related to the person in the mirror affords the therapeutic dyad the opportunity to monitor changes in the self-system as they occur. This work can take place concurrently with efforts to improve problem solving and decision making. The clinician may find that these two treatment strategies indeed complement each other.

However, one cautionary note is warranted, in that the person-in-the-mirror technique *should not* be employed during the acute phase of treatment when there is still an active suicidal crisis. This type of introspective self-examination can be too threatening and dangerous during the crisis stage. If the youth looks at him/herself during the time of active suicidal thoughts and impulses, there may be too much self-hate and an inability to see or experience anything positive. This technique, then, is only suitable after the active suicidal phase has passed (i.e. the therapist feels comfortable in their assessment that the client is no longer actively suicidal).

Ethical and Legal Considerations

The ethical principles for each of the mental health disciplines guide the professional behavior of the practitioner. Each of these codes provide the limits of confidentiality and specify under what conditions confidentiality must be broken. In some cases, not breaking confidentiality can be considered unethical and perhaps negligent. The code of ethics of the American Psychological Association (1990), for example,[3] states that the confidentiality of information obtained from a client must be protected at all times, "except in those unusual circumstances in which to do so would result in clear danger to the person or to others" (p. 636).

In reference to the earlier discussion of negotiating a no-kill contract, the preceeding ethical guideline could conceivably come into play. Specifically, if the clinician does not receive a clear agreement from the client that they will not harm themselves during an agreed period of time and there is a lethal suicide plan with imminent intent, then the clinician incurs the responsibility of breaking confidence in order to secure the physical safety of the client. Once the clinician is forced to break confidentiality, the possibility of the relationship continuing to be therapeutic is dramatically jeopardized. The breaking of confidentiality is, therefore, a last desperate step which should only be exercised after every other alternative has been exhausted. Nevertheless, if the threat is "clear and imminent" with no assurance of client safety, the clinician has to do whatever is necessary to see that the safety of the client is insured. Possible action steps that may be taken include notification of parents, initiation of commitment procedures (involuntary hospitalization), or notification of law enforcement officials. The limits of confidentiality in

---

3. The authors were trained as psychologists, so many of the examples used are based upon American Psychological Association standards or ethical principles.

this situation are not specific to treating suicidal youth but rather apply to all suicidal clients across the age spectrum and involves only one ethical and legal principle: confidentiality.

There are other legal and ethical points that must be considered when working with minors. For example, a minor in treatment is technically not identified as the client. It is the parents, not the minor child, who retain the legal authority to provide the permission for, or refusal of, treatment for their child. In effect, the parents are the client of the care provider although the child is the recipient of treatment. Since parents are legally responsible for the welfare of their children, it is through this responsibility that they become the clients of the provider (Brewer & Faitak, 1989). However, this is counterbalanced by the unique responsibility a psychologist assumes in the treatment of a minor, in that the child is not in the position to grant voluntary informed consent (since this is the prerogative of the parent). Every aspect of treatment must be conducted with the overall welfare of the child in mind. This is specifically noted in the APA code of ethics in principle 5D, which states, "When working with minors or other persons who are unable to give voluntary, informed consent, psychologists take special care to protect these persons' best interests" (p. 636). Thus, the ethical principles guide the behavior of the psychologist in this dual relationship. This ethical code recognizes the legal rights of the parents while guiding the therapist to respect and uphold the rights of the children.

The therapist is then in the ethically precarious position of having to provide information to the parents (to obtain informed consent) while not undermining the therapeutic trust of the client. According to Waltz and Scheuneman (1970), in order to receive informed consent from a legal perspective two criteria must be satisfied: (a) the person (parents) must be aware of the information that he or she is consenting to; and (b) the person's assent must constitute more than mere acquiescence. To satisfy this requirement, the parents have to be informed about treatment objectives and procedures, any potential deleterious effects, the expected length and cost of treatment, and how treatment can be terminated if necessary (Hare-Mustin et al., 1979; Keith-Spiegel & Koocher, 1985).

Parents must be given the opportunity to ask any questions they may have about the evaluation, treatment objectives, or treatment procedures before they can agree to and grant permission for the treatment plan to proceed. It is possible that there may be elements of the plan to which the parents may object. In this situation the clinician has to decide if these elements of the plan to which the parents are objecting are essential to the treatment. If these elements are essential, then the clinician may have to refer the parents to another setting or clinician while trying to also explain once again the treatment rationale to see if the parents will reconsider their objections.

Once the clinician has received the informed consent of the parents, treatment can then begin. The child does not have the right to legally refuse treatment once permission is granted by the parents. However, effective treatment obviously cannot take place without the cooperation of the child. In order to best facilitate the child's treatment, the objectives and treatment plan which were spelled out for the parents should be carefully and as thoroughly explained to the child in language that they will understand. This explanation hopefully fosters the child's alliance and treatment with the clinician by encouraging the child to take an active role in the process. Ross (1974) asserts that children have the *right* to be told the truth, be treated with respect, be taken seriously, and have a meaningful involvement in activities that affect their lives.

Technically, the parents have the right to any and all information obtained in the evaluation or treatment process. However, the clinician must remember that their first obligation is to see to the welfare of the child, and this has to be taken into consideration in terms of information which is shared with the parents. The amount and timing of the disclosure of information must always be linked to the best interests of the child's treatment. In order for treatment to be effective, the child must be able to trust the therapist and be able to share their deepest and most private thoughts. The child needs the assurance that everything they reveal in treatment will not be readily and inappropriately communicated back to the parents. Thus, the therapist has to develop a delicate sense of balance between keeping the parents informed (as a function of their legal rights) while still being respectful of the privacy of the child.

References

Alanen, Y. O., Rinne, R., & Paukkonen, P. (1981). On family dynamics and family therapy in suicidal attempts. *Crisis, 2,* 20–26.

American Psychological Association. (1981). Ethical principles of psychologists. *American Psychologist, 36*(6), 633–638.

Beck, A. J., & Beck, A. T. (1978). Cognitive therapy of depression and suicide. *American Journal of Psychotherapy, 32,* 201–219.

Berman, A. L. (1987). Adolescent suicide. *The Clinical Psychologist,* Fall 1987, 87–91.

Brewer, T., & Faitak, M. T. (1989). Ethical guidelines for the inpatient psychiatric care of children. *Professional Psychology: Research and Practice, 20*(3), 142–147.

Comstock, B., & McDermott, M. (1975). Group therapy for patients who attempt suicide. *International Journal of Group Therapy, 25,* 44–49.

Corder, B. F., & Haizlip, T. M. (1982). Recognizing suicidal behavior in children. *Medical Times,* September, 255–305.

Farberow, N. L. (1976). Group therapy for self-destructive persons. In J. J. Parad, H. P. L. Resnik, & L. G. Parad (Eds.), *Emergency and disaster management: A mental health sourcebook.* Bowie, MD: Charles Press.

Frederick, C. J. (1985). An introduction and overview of youth suicide. In M. L. Peck, N. L. Farberow, & R. E. Litman (Eds.), *Youth suicide* (pp. 1–16). New York: Springer Publishing Co.

Getz, W. L., Allen, D. B., Myers, R. K., & Linder, K. C. (1983). *Brief counseling with suicidal persons.* Lexington, MA: Lexington Books.

Greydanus, D. E., Porter, J., Rypma, C. B., & Heuer, T. (1986). The behavioral medicine unit: A community hospital model for inpatient treatment of adolescent depression. *Seminar in Adolescent Medicine, 2*(4), 311–319.

Hare-Mustin, R. T., Marecek, J., Kaplan, A. G., & Liss-Levinson, N. (1979). Rights of clients, responsibilities of therapists. *American Psychologist, 34,* 3–16.

Hendin, H. (1981). Psychotherapy and suicide. *American Journal of Psychotherapy, 35,* 469–480.

Hipple, J., & Cimbolic, P. (1979). *The counselor and suicidal crisis.* Springfield, IL: Charles C Thomas.

Hipple, J. (1982). Group treatment of suicidal clients. *Journal for Specialists in Group Work, 7,* 245–250.

Hynes, J. J. (1976). An exploratory study of the affective future time perspective of adolescent attempters: Relationship to clinical identification and lethality, and its implications for postvention. *Dissertation Abstracts International, 37,* 1404A–1405A.

Keidel, G. C. (1983). Adolescent suicide. Symposium on adolescent health care. *Nursing Clinics of North America, 18*(2), 323–332.

Keith-Spiegel, P., & Koocher, G. P. (1985). *Ethics in psychology: Professional standards and cases.* New York: Random House.

Levenson, M., & Neuringer, C. Problem-solving behavior in suicidal adolescents. *Journal of Consulting and Clinical Psychology, 37,* 433–436.

Litt, I. F., Cuskey, W. R., & Rudd, S. (1983). Emergency room evaluation of the adolescent who attempts suicide: compliance with follow-up. *Journal of Adolescent Health Care, 4*(2), 106–108.

Motto, J. A. (1985). Treatment concerns in preventing youth suicide. In M. L. Peck, N. L. Farberow, & R. E. Litman (Eds.). *Youth suicide* (91–111). New York: Springer Publishing Co.

Nezu, A. M. (1986). Efficacy of a social problem-solving therapy approach for unipolar depression. *Journal of Consulting & Clinical Psychology, 54,* 196–202.

Nezu, A. M., & Perri, M. G. (1989). Social problem-solving therapy for unipolar depression: An initial dismantling investigation. *Journal of Consulting and Clinical Psychology, 57*(3), 408–413.

Piersma, H. L., & Van Wingen, S. (1988). A hospital-based crisis service for adolescents: A program description. *Adolescence, 23*(90), 491–500.

Platt, J. J., Spivak, G., Altman, N., Altman, D., & Peizer, S. B. (1974). Adolescent problem-solving thinking. *Journal of Consulting and Clinical Psychology, 6,* 787–793.

Richman, J. (1979). Family therapy of attempted suicide. *Family Process, 18,* 131–142.

Richman, J. (1986). *Family therapy for suicidal people.* New York: Springer.

Ross, A. O. (1974). *The rights of children as psychotherapy patients.* Paper presented at the meeting of the American Psychological Association, New Orleans: LA, September.

Shrier, D. K. (1987). Teenage suicide: Causes, warning signs, and interventions. *New Jersey Medicine, 84*(5), 339–343.

Toolin, J. M. (1962). Suicide and suicide attempters in children and adolescents. *American Journal of Psychiatry, 118,* 719–724.

Walker, B. A., & Mehr, M. (1983). Adolescent suicide—a family crisis: A model for effective intervention by family therapists. *Adolescence, 18*(70), 286–292.

Waltz, J., & Scheuneman, T. (1970). Informed consent to therapy. *Northwestern University Law Review, 64,* 628–650.

Chapter 5

SURVIVORS OF SUICIDE: UNDERSTANDING AND COPING WITH THE LEGACY OF SELF-INFLICTED DEATH

Ellen S. Zinner, PsyD.

Introduction

Suicidologist Edwin Shneidman (1984) writes that "the suicidal person leaves his psychological skeleton in the survivor's closet" (p. 69). These words are both dramatic and accurate. Initially, survivors seem to stare at the "skeleton," their minds fixed on the event and its immediate aftermath. They stand there immobilized with one hand on the doorknob. And, for many months, the door will not close. With much time and pain, the closet door does shut, only to pop open again at the mention of a particular name or place or anniversary date.

The skeleton never really goes away. Shneidman notes that these survivor-victims have lost their inalienable right to lead unstigmatized lives. If a parent had committed suicide decades ago, the "specialness," the awfulness of this particular mode of death, exists long after the pain has lessened. The survivor need only be asked in passing how the parent's death occurred for the skeleton to rattle once more.

This chapter will examine several areas relevant to suicide survivorship in an attempt to sensitize professionals and lay persons attempting to support survivors. Initially, this chapter will examine the fundamental nature of suicide bereavement—who are survivor-victims and what are the unique characteristics of being a survivor of suicide loss? The focus will then shift to a consideration of typical responses of suicide survivor-victims, both emotionally and behaviorally. Finally, this chapter will provide treatment suggestions helpful in dealing with suicide survivors.

It should be noted before preceding, however, that research on suicide survivorship has been relatively scant, considering the rapid development of suicidology over the last thirty years. Primary focus in the field has been on the self-destructive individual, identification and intervention. "Of some twenty-two hundred works on suicide that had been published since 1965—books, articles, reports in professional journals, theses—only a handful even mentioned the effects of suicide upon survivors" (Lukas & Seiden, 1987, p. 4). While preventing suicides certainly speaks to the problem of survivorship, the annual suicide total of some 29,000+ deaths nonetheless leaves an estimated 200,000+ anguished individuals in its wake. The needs and responses of these survivors must be understood and addressed.

More recently, a small but growing body of research on survivor-victims has been developing (Foglia, 1984; McIntosh, 1985–86). Much of this valuable information is presented anecdotally or is based on clinical case studies of small numbers of patients. While useful, these writings do not emphasize other kinds of adaptive responses of individuals who do not find themselves in treatment (and therefore not within "clinical" samples). Further, only a few studies have utilized appropriate control groups for comparison of responses with non-suicide survivors or have gone beyond interview data to more standardized measures (e.g. McNeil et al., 1988). A weakness, too, has been in not studying the social interactions of survivors within their primary network. The bulk of this chapter will rely on clinical and field data citing as frequently as possible research studies to support these observations.

Nature of Suicide Bereavement

In their bereavement, are survivor-victims of suicide significantly different from survivors who have experienced the death of loved ones from other modes of death? Are they condemned to a life forever disrupted by the suicide event? The answer from a clinical perspective and recent empirical data is no to both questions.

While survivor-victims may consider themselves to have more severe grief, indirect measures reveal symptoms consistent with bereavement effects from other sudden-death circumstances (Maddison, 1968; Shepherd & Barraclough, 1974; Rudestam, 1977a). The McNeil et al. study (1988), comparing widow survivors of suicide and of accidental deaths, for instance, reports little difference among these surviving wives with respect to standardized assessment of family functioning, life stress, and psychiatric symptomatology within the first two years of bereavement.

Both groups demonstrated clinically significant levels of symptoms, however, reflecting Parkes's (1965) view of grief as a "functional mental disorder." Indeed, it may well be the predominant factor of suddenness that precipitates a difficult mourning process. Several researchers have noted the inability to psychologically prepare for loss to be a major factor in the intensity of the initial shock and in coming to terms with the loss (Lindemann, 1944; Woolsey et al., 1978; Vachon et al., 1982).

Clearly, being a suicide survivor can have devastating and long-lasting effects on one's development and well-being (Cain, 1978; Calhoun et al., 1980). Yet, there are limited studies and clinical observations which indicate that there are indeed "non-pathologic" survivors of suicide with successful coping capabilities. Especially where the relationship between the survivor and the deceased had been a positive one, where the cause of death is attributed to circumstances outside the control of the survivor, and where opportunities to have prevented the death are seen as negligible, effective adaptive defenses can and have been demonstrated (Augenbraum & Neuringer, 1972; Henslin, 1972). Those survivors who continue to deny aspects of the suicide in the face of conflicting data, who view the death as a stigma to themselves and their family, or who have come to see the death as courageous, have a more difficult time adjusting to the loss. Also, survivors who discover the body have a particularly difficult adjustment (Rudestam, 1977a).

In Rudestam's 1977 study of various relatives of the deceased, severe and enduring physical and emotional reactions among some individual survivors were found, but increased strengthening of family relations was also noted. He concludes that, within the first six months of the loss, "it does not appear that relationships within the family have deteriorated or become destructive, but, if anything, the relationships may actually be strengthened as values are re-examined and members share a common plight" (p. 170).

In sum, research suggests that there are mitigating factors in the adjustment process of a survivor-victim. Social and personal recuperation certainly are reflective of the survivor's unique personality, experiences, and coping abilities (Fulton, 1978). In addition to factors mentioned above, the relationship between the survivor and the deceased, and the extent of unfinished business, enter into the grief equation. Survivors for whom the suicide is less role disruptive and who have more outside resources also are more likely to adapt to the suicide (Demi, 1978). Finally, anticipation of the suicide, acknowledged by a substantial minority of survivors, can lessen the impact and positively contribute to a self-supporting interpretation of the death and is frequently seen as one of the most important factors influencing adequacy of recovery (Sheskin & Wallace, 1976; Doka, 1984–85).

Unique Characteristics of Suicide Loss

Perhaps attempting to assess the impact of a suicide on a close survivor is somewhat akin to debating whether losing an arm or a leg is more dysfunctional. A suicide death, like any significant loss, makes a major assault on one's well-being and life perspective. There are some relatively unique features of a suicide loss, however, that color the postmortem period and interventionists should be aware of these.

SUDDENNESS OF LOSS. Already mentioned is the suddenness of the loss which preclude any of the potentially beneficial aspects of anticipatory grief discussed in the literature (Lindemann, 1944; Woolsey et al., 1978; Vachon et al., 1982).

SOCIAL STIGMA. Another factor is the social stigma attached to this mode of death. Stephenson (1985) speaks to "a lack of an explanation for the suicide, coupled with the fear and loathing of an outrageous death [that] places the survivors in a stigmatized position in American society" (p. 190). Calhoun, Selby, and Faulstich (1980) compared the reactions of 119 adults to fictitious accounts of a child's death from several modes of death. When the child was to have died by suicide, the parents were less respected and more frequently blamed for the child's death. The child was also perceived as being more severely disturbed prior to the death. Rudestam and Imbroll's 1983 study supports this result, too.

In an extension and elaboration of the Calhoun et al. study, Reynolds and Cimbolic (1988–89) examined the attitudes toward various suicide survivors of 60 college students responding to fictionalized case histories of the suicide of a child, spouse, and parent. Half of the study participants were given an article on suicide to read prior to exposure to the case histories in an attempt to evaluate whether "suicide education" influences subject attitude. Results indicated that such educational efforts did little to change the predominantly negative views held toward survivors. Additionally, adult survivors were less liked, found to be more blameworthy, and generated more anger and avoidance reactions than did child survivors.

Clinical research has shown stigma to be a major stressor on suicide survivors when compared to non-suicide survivors (Wallace, 1973; Demi,

1978). Interestingly, many survivors do not report that they feel stigmatized (Solomon, 1982–83), and those that do often speak of having heard gossip and having experienced negative interactions with official agents (Shepherd & Barraclough, 1974). Given the frequent use of denial and the tendency to limit information concerning the suicide to outsiders, the question of how many survivors actually see themselves freed from cultural stigma needs further investigation (Stephenson, 1985). Changing norms regarding more understanding views toward suicide could lessen the impact of this factor (Droogas et al., 1982–83; Boldt, 1982–83).

SHAME. Society has held such clearly negative views about suicide that both the deceased and those close to him or her frequently share in the social castigation. Because this is so pervasive, it is difficult to dismiss this feeling of being stigmatized if one is a suicide survivor.

OFFICIAL INVESTIGATIONS. With a suicide comes official investigations by police and sometimes insurance representatives. Rarely are these encounters pleasant or supportive for survivors. The needs of the families and the needs of the investigators often seem to be at odds during these interactions. The standard vocabulary of police personnel which includes "securing the scene of the crime" and "seizing the suicide note as evidence" often appears menacing and cold.

LACK OF SOCIAL SUPPORT. Lack of support from relatives and friends is often experienced by survivors in the wake of a suicide. Only half of the subjects in Rudestan's (1977a) study of family survivors said friends were helpful and willing to listen. Silverman (1972) also notes minimal support and sees this as "an additional estrangement," not only from family, but from the larger community as well, which differentiates the suicide survivor from survivors of other modes of death. One reason for this may be sheer awkwardness. Frequently asked is what is the "proper" thing to say at a funeral or to a newly bereaved individual. If it is difficult to face a person in grief when the death has more "social respectability," then it is little wonder that a suicide leaves many even less prepared.

VOLITIONAL ASPECT. Lastly, the seeming volition of suicide tends to intensify the feelings of rejection and confusion in the survivor (Schuyler, 1979). The all-too-human query of "why" did this tragedy happen, common to all loss situations, is not readily or satisfactorily answered. Suicide notes are left only in the minority of deaths, and even these often do not provide the kind of understanding needed. Answers to the questions of "What?" "Why?" and "Why me?" will plague the survivor-victim throughout the mourning period and beyond, especially so when it is a youthful suicide.

Emotional and Behavioral Responses

Guilt

An almost expected response for survivor-victims is a feeling of guilt. Guilt may be hard to avoid with no other "easy" or external cause to blame for the death like an illness or accident. Henslin (1972, p. 219) writes that "the category into which one is taught to place such deaths determine how one will define the death, including especially the 'cause' of the death and one's role or possible role in that death. Guilt does not originate in 'objective' situations, but in the perception of the individual."

Feelings of guilt may be increased where conflict or isolation within the family has preceded the suicide. Suicides sometimes occur where everything seemed to be going well. Such deaths can come as a total surprise for the significant others involved. But, more common, familial harmony has not existed and there were strains in relationships often for some time. A teenager may have been isolating himself or herself for months, upstairs in the bedroom with the music blaring. What may have been considered a "phase" becomes a nightmare when suicide is the outcome. Surviving parents may feel guilt because the guns or pills used in the suicide were available in the home, complicated by the feelings of "I should have done something."

Some survivors feel guilty in believing that they should have seen clues indicating suicidal intention. Sometimes there were warning signs, and such indicators are more obvious following the death when their significance becomes apparent. One friend mentions records given away; a sister will recall a morbid remark. Suddenly, such diverse clues fit together to form a tight picture of self-destruction. Even when the guilt is not legitimate, survivors are torn enough and despondent enough to create it.

Anger

Anger is another response typically experienced by survivor-victims during the grieving process. Such feelings are easy to comprehend because survivors must contend with a whole new set of problems caused by the suicide. The anger may be directed at society for its pressures and flaws that seem to encourage suicidal actions and yet which condemns its members and those around them who dare take their lives. The anger may be turned inward for having been a real or imagined accomplice to the suicide. The anger may be aimed at any one of a number of forces— God, teachers, counselors, the peer group—who seemed to have failed the deceased when they were needed most. Or, as is most often the case, the anger may be directed at the victim for having taken such desperate action that caused so much pain for the survivors.

Certainly there are cases of bizarre family relationships and perhaps even more situations where blatant cries for help have not been heeded. Nevertheless, it is important to emphasize that no one else pulled the trigger; no one else swallowed the pills; no one else tied the rope that led to the death except the suicide victim. The responsibility for the death must lie with the individual now buried.

Anger at the deliberateness of the suicide and the awfulness of the consequences is justified and needs to be confronted and expressed. Many times anger doesn't feel "nice" and doesn't sound "nice," and grievers may have no safe place to vent their true emotions. Consequently, survivors may become stuck in their anger, unable to move on to other feelings or tasks in their grief work, Often, too, survivors may become "hooked" by certain details of the "suicide script." That is, some aspect of the circumstances surrounding the suicide may be especially troubling and may repeat itself over and over in their mind. For example, the method, location, notoriety, or timing of a suicide death (as well as circumstances surrounding discovery of the body) may leave deep survivor scars. These barbed pieces of the story may seem insignificant to others, but, because of a particular detail of the suicide script, survivors may continue to flounder in their attempts to put the whole suicide event into a perspective or understanding with which they can live.

Relief

A completely different reaction to suicide is relief. Not "nice," perhaps, but real and understandable in situations where the actions and moods of the deceased have been disruptive to the family. It is not unusual to see an entire family having problems because of the alcoholism, drug abuse, or acting-out behavior of one dysfunctional member. Where suicidal threats and attempts have been a frequent occurrence, the completed act may be met with thoughts of "at least it's over." The unhappiness experienced for too long a time may be put to rest along with the deceased. Sharing these honest feelings, however, is difficult and socially unwelcomed. Expressing or even having thoughts of relief over the suicide may lead to feelings of additional guilt (Rando, 1984).

Denial

Survivors also use denial as a defense mechanism when a suicide has occurred, since the reality of this manner of death causes so much pain. While denial can be beneficial in initially buffering the impact of the loss (Woolsey et al., 1978), it can have long-term negative consequences for successful grief work (Dorpat, 1972). If a note is not left or discovered, there may be room for doubt and denial. Indeed, an accidental overdose or gun accident or even a murder could have taken place, despite clues to the contrary. What happens more often than not, however, is that one member of the family will "hold out," believing that something other than suicide must have taken place. Other family members are seen as betraying the good reputation and memory of the deceased. Family support in their mutual loss and grief is all but destroyed.

Denial can also be used to reject the reasons that a suicide took place. A survivor may ignore the reasoning of a suicide note and decide that the real motives for the suicide had to do with pressures entirely different than those stated. Or the family may deny any kind of rejection and see the suicide as a noble gesture, one designed to protect the family from the continued failures or misbehaviors of the deceased. Unfortunately, "denial is among the most vulnerable of defenses because of its blatant attempt to counteract reality and is the most readily assaulted by reality" (Neuringer, 1977, p. 42).

Search for Meaning

Common to suicide survivors, too, is a desperate search for meaning, an atempt to understand the "why" behind the self-destruction. The "why's" and "what if's" parade constantly through the minds of survivors, and various answers and scenarios are tried on, then discarded, in the effort. The answer rarely comes with clarity sufficient for the lasting satisfaction of the survivor. At best, the lament of "why" comes up less frequently, less insistently, until survivors eventually resign themselves to not knowing.

Views of Afterlife

Religious beliefs can affect the meaning of suicide. For example, it is a traditional Christian view that self-destruction is sinful and leads to condemnation. The belief that a loved one was troubled enough to take their own life in addition to the belief that censure from God for all eternity brings little comfort or peace to the bereaved.

Even the controversial new perspectives concerning afterlife that stems from the recounts of those who have had near-death experiences does little to relieve this gloomy picture. Some of the stories in Moody's book, *Life After Life* (1975), and other similar materials portray those who have died by suicide as being terribly saddened at their belated awareness of missed opportunities in life.

It should be noted, however, that some views of religious damnation have begun to change. Recent Catholic teachings, for example, view suicide as a human tragedy where the "sinfulness" of the tragic victim should not be judged by the Church (Friday, 1988). Clearly, the Church views suicide as a serious objective evil, going against the basic instinct for self-preservation. But as Friday (1988) discusses, whether the act is an accurate sign of refusing the love and/or sovereignty of God is not clear. While de-emphasizing the sinful aspects of suicide, the emphasis has distinctly shifted to see suicide as a misguided form of tragic behavior.

Blame

Survivors sometimes search for a scapegoat, someone or something to blame, and direct their anger so that the brunt of their wrath stops clear of the deceased and of themselves. It is perhaps easiest to blame the primary caretakers, but onto whom might the primary caretakers lay fault? Drugs, permissiveness, heavy-metal music, sin, society, or pressures of job or school are places for blame. Therapists, physicians, and other health professionals involved in the prevention and intervention effort are easy and frequently chosen targets for finger pointing. God is another force brought into the picture. Survivors often want to know where God's protection and love were when their family member or friend was in need. Sometimes any or all of the above-named targets may be seen as contributing agents in the suicide picture. The point to be made is that survivors may direct all of their negative feelings defensively and prejudicially at one of the above targets to the disruption of the grieving process by repressing or denying their own feelings of responsibility. In the immediate picture, there is "safety" for the survivor in this deflection.

Social Isolation

Social isolation, self-inflicted or not, is a behavior pattern not uncommon among survivors. Some survivors feel so uncomfortable around others that they choose to stay close to home for long periods of time. It is not unusual to see survivors sell homes and change jobs, presumably to get away from the perceived stigma of the death. Further, a certain amount of enforced isolation is a consequence of others' discomfort in interacting with a grieving survivor. Parents often complain that extended family and friends alike rarely mention their dead child's name, as if he or she never existed. Parents cannot and do not want to forget and, more often than not, are grateful to the few friends of their dead child brave enough to come around and reminisce.

Identification with the Deceased

An interesting phenomenon that can occur is identification with the deceased, especially for youthful survivors. It is not uncommon to hear young people express fears that they are so much like the deceased in behavior and coping styles that they feared that they, too, could eventually end up killing themselves one day. In truth, a "coping" technique is being taught by the deceased, and role modeling of the method employed is frequently seen in families with multiple suicides over generations (Danto, 1977b).

Suicidal Behaviors

Lastly, suicide ideation and attempts are other reactions to the pain of the loss and its consequences (Schuyler, 1979). It is fairly normal to think about suicide in times of severe stress or grief. These normal thoughts become more real and threatening, however, when they have been elicited by another's suicide death. Rather than confront the long process of healing, suicide may seem a quick and now chooseable alternative. Survivors must be clearly informed of their vulnerability to suicide in order to prepare them, if possible, for the dark feelings that may overwhelm them.

Helping Suicide Survivor-Victims

Recalling to mind Shneidman's statement at the beginning of this chapter, the skeleton stays in the closet forever. In time, the survivor may open the door less frequently to stare at it. Reaching an acceptable level of reconciliation, however, need not be a solitary or chance journey. Postvention efforts, "consisting of activities that reduce the aftereffects of a traumatic event in the lives of the survivors [can be introduced] to help survivors live longer, more productively, and less stressfully than they are likely to do otherwise" (Shneidman, 1984, p. 413). How, then, can an individual or a group of survivors be helped and supported through an extended period of questioning and pain?

Identifying the Survivor

On a fundamental level, helping survivors requires a preliminary awareness of *who* are survivors of suicide. There are of course a number of obvious survivors—the victim's immediate and extended family, boyfriends/girlfriends, as well as peer-group friends. Nevertheless, there are additional survivors of a youthful suicide who may be less obvious. These may include mental health professionals, first responders to the scene of death (e.g. police and emergency medical workers), and even whole groups (e.g. a school class or a church youth group). Zinner's (1985) notion of "group survivorship" conceptualizes groups as extended families which must mourn the loss of a member. Effective responses to survivors therefore must fundamentally begin with fundamental identification of who may be grieving the suicide death.

Helpful Responses to Suicide

LEARNING ABOUT SUICIDE. Survivors, first of all, can help themselves. They can inform themselves about what has happened and what they may expect in their grieving. Even though articles frequently appear in newspapers and magazines, survivors find themselves woefully naive on the subject of suicide when it invades their life. Becoming familiar with suicide statistics, theories, and clues may help survivors develop their own perspective on what is known, and this may help them in dealing with their grief. Many informative and well-written books have been published about death in general (Shneidman, 1984; Stephenson, 1985; DeSpelder and Strickland, 1987) and specifically about suicide and suicide survivorship (Hewett, 1980; Hatton & Valente, 1984; Lukas & Seiden, 1987).

No two people may grieve exactly alike, and no amount of information will take away all the pain. But enough people have grieved and enough grievers have been studied for symptoms and patterns common to bereavement to be identified (Worden, 1982; Parkes & Weiss, 1983; Rando, 1984). Foreknowledge of these patterns may reduce the fear and anxiety aroused when a survivor encounters a normal aspect of grief for the first time. Believing that you have actually seen a deceased person, who is deeply yearned for, is a fairly common experience.

ACKNOWLEDGING FEELINGS. Survivors can also support themselves by acknowledging their feelings and finding avenues for expressing those emotions. Betsey Ross (1983), in her excellent booklet entitled *After Suicide: A Unique Process,* says it clearly when she writes: "claim your right to grieve." Survivors are in pain, and they have the right and the need to respond to their loss. Crying is one naturally given means for the expression of sadness and pain. In our culture, that avenue has been blocked with restrictions on where, when and for whom the crying may take place. Sometimes survivors accept these restrictions as natural and are unable to tear down barriers when tears would be most helpful. The bereaved need to give themselves and others permission to express their grief. Anger, too, needs to be vented in a constructive manner. Redirecting hurt onto others only creates new problems with which to contend. Guilt, already discussed, is another emotion that needs to be examined and expressed. In this area, the guilt generated is often largely out of proportion to any feelings of unmet responsibility. But the guilt which remains after an honest appraisal of one's contribution to the suicide decision must be faced and accepted (Rando, 1985). Holding on to guilt keeps survivors attached to the suicide and serves as a self-inflicted punishment. It is not uncommon to see survivors "paying off" or atoning for their guilt by becoming active in suicide prevention and intervention efforts, such as volunteering at crisis hot lines, assisting at survivor groups, or giving presentations at schools and churches. This may be a healthy sublimation.

REFRAMING. Lastly, survivors can ultimately help themselves to deal with the suicide loss by finding an acceptable placement of the event within the framework of their own life (Schuyler, 1979). By this is meant two things: survivors need to find a *functional interpretation* of the meaning of the suicide act, and they need to develop functional *consequences* of its having occurred. There may be many reasons why individuals take their lives and many ways of interpreting their actions. Even a detailed suicide note cannot tell the whole story because there are subconscious motivations and influences underlying the decision. So, if survivors can never really know why someone commits suicide, they are free to settle on a "reasonable" interpretation or understanding that supports rather than condemns them.

Instructive here is Iris Bolton's 1984 book, *My Son, My Son,* about the suicide of her son, Mitch. Mitch shot himself in the head using two guns. Imagine how any mother might interpret such action. Bolton believes that Mitch had come to the decision to die without any reservations and that he used two guns to avoid any possibility of not fulfilling his plan to die. His method of death reflected his certainty, and his actions left no room for his mother or anyone else to intervene. Bolton's interpretation clearly gives responsibility to her son. It is an understanding that she can *live* with.

Developing functional consequences suggests finding some value in the suicide. Finding good in what is an awful and wasteful act may sound absurd at first glance. But the truth is that no amount of anger or guilt or grieving can undo the deed. What can be a difference in the lives of survivors, however, is "making meaning," finding some kind of personal or social compensation related to the suicide. Many parent survivors, as mentioned before, have volunteered their time and monies to education efforts in the death field and have even changed careers into the helping professions because of the suicide in their personal life history. Survivors need not create these positive consequences publicly or dramatically. Any perceived change or contribution that took inception from the death can be interpreted as a meaningful consequence.

SUPPORT BY OTHERS. Professional interveners, fellow survivors, or concerned friends can also help survivor-victims in their grieving. They can provide the safe place and patient ear to those who need to tell the story over and over again. Most survivors have a great need to repeat the details of events leading up to the suicide as well as the finding of the body and the post-death rituals. This is reality testing, which functions to psychologically confirm a fact which we might prefer to deny. This can eventually be boring and frustrating for the listener. Professionals are trained and paid to listen to the necessary recapitulations; friends must rely on their own compassion and patience. For most survivors, having supportive friends and family may be all that they need during their period of mourning.

Grief work has few shortcuts and is longer than most expect or our culture allows. In a mutual help group for survivors a few years ago, a fairly new member, whose daughter had hanged herself two months before, asked, "How long will the pain continue?" The group responded most seriously to the gentleman's question, and, together, related their experience that it was not until the third year following the suicide of their children that their lives took on a sense of normalcy again. Indeed, this group expressed the feeling that the second year of grieving was even harder for them than the first. During the first year following the death, survivors expect to be deeply pained by every holiday, anniversary, and memory associated with the deceased. After the first death anniversary has passed, however, many survivors believe the worst to be over. They are less steeled, less prepared for the blow of a second Christmas and a second birthday without the family member or friend.

MENTAL HEALTH PROFESSIONALS. Professional interventionists may be of great benefit to survivors unable to cope with the length or depth of their grief. Empathic listening by a trained stranger may be exactly what the bereaved individual needs. When anger is blocked or repressed, for example, a counselor might ask a survivor to describe what he or she could be angry about with respect to the deceased. Using the "empty chair" technique, a counselor may ask a client to talk to the suicide victim as if the deceased were sitting with them. The professional invites the survivor to say all those things left unsaid and to express directly to the deceased whatever feelings the death has engendered. Sometimes the client might be encouraged to sit in the empty chair to respond as the victim himself might to what is being communicated. This kind of role playing can be very powerful and very effective.

FORMAL AND INFORMAL RITUALS. Of particular benefit to survivors in the early stages of grieving is the funeral ceremony. The funeral is a leave-taking ceremony, designed not only to dispose of the body in a culturally and religiously acceptable manner but to support the bereaved in a time-appropriate and concrete way. Not all funerals do this, but all funerals hold that potential. For any funeral situation (and especially where the death has been by suicide), family and friends need to be able to mourn their loss in a normal and expected fashion (Grollman, 1971; Rando, 1984; Doka, 1984–85).

Emphasis should be on the life lived as well as on the tragedy of the death. This can be accomplished by the creation of a "memory table," for instance, at the funeral home or church (Ross, 1983). The memory table can be used to arrange pictures and items belonging to or reminiscent of the victim and thus provides a more positive (living) focus for family and friends in mourning.

Funerals are also vehicles for the awareness and expression of feelings. They present an opportunity for letters containing thoughts unsaid to be written down and placed in the casket. Personal tokens can also be placed with the body, an action that might have great meaning for the survivor and which may well serve to support later grief resolution.

Anniversaries and other special days offer similar opportunities to confront in a meaningful and positive way the loss that has occurred. Birthdays, holidays, and the death anniversary day will never be the same again. Ignoring them or hiding from them does not reduce the pain that they can elicit. "Celebrating" them, acknowledging the occasion, is at once more healthy and helpful.

MUTUAL HELP GROUPS. Survivors need to re-enter life and the company of the living during their long bereavement period. Mutual help groups for survivors are a good place for this re-entry to take place. More and more survivor groups are being organized each year. Names include Survivors of Suicide (SOS), SEASONS, Safeplace, and Ray of Hope, among many others. A national listing of these groups is available through the American Association of Suicidology (2459 S. Ash, Denver, Colorado, 80222).

While suicide support groups are growing in number, their effectiveness is based more or anecdotal than research evidence thus far (Zinner, 1986). A limited number of studies published on mutual help groups serving members who have experienced a significant death loss reveal relatively mild involvement or commitment of members to the group reflected in a relatively short period of membership and, consequently, high member turnover (Katz, 1981; Gottleib, 1982). Members show greater expressed attitudinal than behavioral changes, and they attribute much credit for these changes to outside social networking developed from group contacts.

A 1982 panel survey of parents bereaved less than eighteen months found no difference in depression as measured on objective or projective tests over a one-year period regardless of membership in a survivor support group. Yet, parents most involved in a bereavement group expressed a positive personal change over the time period (Videka-

Sherman, 1982). A follow-up study, comparing parent survivors involved in psychotherapy versus those involved in mutual help groups only, found no evidence of impact of either modality on specific indices of mental health or parental or marital role functioning. Attitude changes were again noted, however, with respect to problems encountered by bereaved parents.

Interestingly, those parents who chose either professional or mutual help support were found to be initially more depressed, more anxious, to have lower self-esteem, less life satisfaction and less sense of personal mastery than a comparison group of bereaved parents who had not sought outside help. Women were found to be more depressed than men, and parents whose children died suddenly and unexpectedly remained depressed longer. Again, negative or findings of no difference on assessment instruments *did not* reflect the positive experiences expressed by bereaved parents in mutual help groups. Members reported directly and on semantic differential scales the benefits accrued from group membership (Videka-Sherman & Lieberman, 1985).

Suicide survivor groups are a good supportive resource for those in grief because they are *socially acceptable*. Unfortunately, in our culture, therapy and counseling are considered stigmatizing by many and chosen by relatively few. Grief is a normal and natural reaction to loss and, for many survivors, does not require therapeutic intervention. Attending a mutual help group does not label someone as "sick" but rather as "in need" of giving and receiving support. In these groups, bereaved individuals can find *real understanding and empathy* which normalizes feelings that may appear alien and bizarre (Danto, 1977; Hatten & Valente, 1984). No matter what feeling or behavior is expressed, there are always people nodding their head in affirmation, assuring that they, too, know what this experience is like. Survivor groups are not meant to replace therapy. But they are indeed therapeutic and provide important models of surviving. In the survivor group, there is proof that life goes on.

Conclusion

This chapter has been about the legacy of self-inflicted death. Research into the range and depth of the impact of this type of sudden death and into ways of developing coping capabilities is still forthcoming. Interventionists for their part need to be sensitive to the ripple effect of suicide in order to identify all survivor-victims in need of support.

Recognizing the special features of this type of loss is helpful in understanding the emotional and behavioral responses that are common to survivor-victims. While it is clear that survivors can and do cope with this awful legacy, education and training of both survivors and interventionists can only facilitate the grief work survivors must undertake.

References

Augenbraum, B., & Neuringer, C. (1972). Helping survivors with the impact of a suicide. In A. Cain (Ed.), *Survivors of suicide*. Springfield, Illinois: Charles C Thomas.

Boldt, M. (1982–83). Normative evaluations of suicide and death: A cross-generational study. *Omega, 13*, 145–157.

Bolton, I. (1984). *My Son, My Son* (2nd ed.). Atlanta: Bolton Press.

Calhoun, L.. Shelby, J., & Faulstich, M. (1980). Reactions to the parents of the child suicide. *Journal of Consulting and Clinical Psychology, 48*, 535–536.

Danto, B. L. (1977a). Family survivors of suicide. In B. L. Danto and A. H. Kutscher (Eds.), *Suicide and bereavement*. New York: MSS Information.

Danto, B. L. (1977b). Project SOS: Volunteers in action with survivors of suicide. In B. L. Danto and A. H. Kutscher (Eds.), *Suicide and bereavement*. New York: MSS Information.

Demi, A. (1978). Adjustment to widowhood after sudden death: Suicide and nonsuicide survivors compared. *Communicating Nursing Research, 11*, 91–99.

DeSpelder, L. A., & Strickland, A. L. (1987). *The last dance* (2nd ed.). Palo Alto, California: Mayfield.

Dorpat, T. L. (1972). Psychological effects of parental suicide on surviving children. In A. Cain (Ed.), *Survivors of suicide*. Springfield, Illinois: Charles C Thomas.

Droogas, A., Siter, R., & O'Connell, A. (1982–83). Effects of personal and situational factors on attitudes toward suicide. *Omega, 13*, 127–144.

Foglia, B. B. (1984). Survivor-victims of suicide. In C. L. Hatton and S. M. Valente (Eds.), *Suicide: Assessment and intervention* (2nd ed.). Norwalk, Connecticut: Appleton-Century-Crofts.

Fulton, R. L. (1978). Death, grief, and social recuperation. *Omega, 1*, 23–28.

Friday, R. (1988). Ask Father Friday. *The Tower Newspaper* (December 2, 1988). Washington, D.C.: Catholic University of America.

Gottlieb, B. H. (1982). Mutual-help groups: Members' views of their benefits and the roles for professional. *Prevention in Human Services, 1*, 55–67.

Grollman, E. A. (1971). *Suicide: Prevention, intervention, postvention*. Boston: Beacon Press.

Henslin, J. (1972). Strategies of adjustment: An ethnomethodological approach to the study of guilt and suicide. In A. Cain (Ed.), *Survivors of suicide*. Springfield, Illinois: Charles C Thomas.

Hatton, E. L., & Valente, S. M. (1984). *Suicide: Assessment and intervention* (2nd ed.). Norwalk, Connecticut: Appleton-Century-Crofts.

Hewett, J. H. (1980). *After suicide.* Philadelphia: Westminster Press.

Katz, A. (1981). Self-help and mutual aid: An emerging social movement. *Annual Review of Sociology, 7,* 129–155.

Lindemann, E. (1944). Symptomatology and management of acute grief. *American Journal of Psychiatry, 101,* 141–148.

Lukas, C., & Seiden, H. M. (1987). *Silent grief: Living in the wake of suicide.* New York: MacMillan.

Maddison, D. (1968). The relevance of conjugal bereavement for preventive psychiatry. *British Journal of Medical Psychology, 41,* 223–233.

McIntosh, J. L. (1985–86). Survivors of suicide: A comprehensive bibliography. *Omega, 16,* 355–370.

McNeil, D. E., Hatcher, C., & Reubin, R. (1988). Family survivors of suicide and accidental death: Consequences for widows. *Suicide and Life-Threatening Behavior, 18,* 137–148.

Moody, R. (1975). *Life after life.* Covington, Georgia: Mockingbird Books.

Parkes, C. (1965). Bereavement and mental illness. *British Journal of Medical Psychology, 38,* 1–26.

Rando, T. A. (1984). *Grief, dying, and death: Clinical interventions for caregivers.* Champaign, IL: Research Press.

Rando, T. A. (1985). Creating psychotherapeutic rituals in the psychotherapy of the bereaved. *Psychotherapy, 22,* 236–240.

Reynolds, F. M., & Cimbolic, P. (1988–89). Attitudes toward suicide survivors as a function of survivors' relationship to the victims. *Omega, 19,* 127–135.

Ross, E. B. (1983). *After suicide: A unique grief process.* Springfield, Illinois: Creative Marketing, Inc.

Rudestam, K. E. (1977a). Physical and psychological responses to suicide in the family. *Journal of Consulting and Clinical Psychology, 45,* 162–170.

Rudestam, K. E. (1977b). The impact of suicide among the young. *Essence, 1,* 221–224.

Rudestam, K. E., & Imbroll, D. (1983). Societal reactions to a child's death by suicide. *Journal of Consulting and Clinical Psychology, 51,* 461–462.

Schuyler, D. (1979). Counseling suicide survivors. *Omega, 4,* 313–321.

Sheskin, A., & Wallace, S. E. (1976). Differing bereavement: Suicide, natural, and accidental death. *Omega, 7,* 229–242.

Shepherd, D., & Barraclough, B. (1974). The aftermath of suicide. *British Journal of Psychiatry, 129,* 267–276.

Shneidman, E. S. (1984). Postvention and the survivor-victim. In E. S. Shneidman (ed.), *Death: Current perspectives* (3rd ed.). Palo Alto, California: Mayfield.

Silverman, P. R. (1972). Intervention with the widow of a suicide. In A. Cain (Ed.), *Survivors of suicide.* Springfield, Illinois: Charles C Thomas.

Soloman, M. (1982–83). The bereaved and the stigma of suicide. *Omega, 13,* 377–387.

Stephenson, J. S. (1985). *Death, grief, and mourning.* New York: The Free Press.

Suicide Prevention Center, Inc. (1983). *Suicide and self-help: Do it yourself guidelines.* Dayton, Ohio: Author.

Vachon, M. L., Rogers, J., Lyall, W. A., Lancee, W. J., Sheldon, A., & Freeman, S.

(1982). Predictors and correlates of adaptation to conjugal bereavement. *American Journal of Psychiatry, 139,* 998–1002.

Videka-Sherman, L. (1982). Effects of participation in a self-help group for bereaved parents: Compassionate friends. *Prevention in Human Services, 1,* 69–77.

Wallace, S. E. (1973). *After suicide.* New York: Poseidon Press.

Woolsey, S. F., Thorton, D. S., & Friedman, S. B. (1978). Sudden death. In O. J. Sahler (Ed.), *The child and death.* St. Louis: C. V. Mosby.

Zinner, E. (1985). Group survivorship: A model and case study application. In E. Zinner (Ed.), *Coping with death on campus: New directions in student services, 31,* 51–68.

Zinner, E. (1986). The mutual help movement: Focus on suicide survivor groups. Unpublished manuscript, Virginia Consortium for Professional Psychology, Norfolk, Virginia.

Zinner, E. (1987). Responding to suicide in schools: A case study in loss intervention and group survivorship. *Journal of Counseling and Development, 65,* 499–501.

Chapter 6

PREVENTING YOUTH SUICIDE: WHAT WORKS? PROGRAM AND POLICY CHOICES FOR SCHOOLS

Cheryl J. Vince, Ed.M. and Kimberly R. Hamrick, M.P.H.[4]

Introduction

"I can't believe the life circumstances and problems of students coming through our doors today," said Thomas Trevisani, an English teacher at Arlington High School in Massachusetts. "They are so much different and far more serious than what we used to see twenty years ago." A large majority of school administrators agreed in a 1985 survey that today's students carry a growing burden of stress. Administrators say that the growing incidence of emotional and academic problems, antisocial behavior, and suicides prove their point (Pine, 1985).

The death of a young person by his or her own hand: there are few events that evoke such feelings of helplessness and failure in us all. What could have been done to prevent this act? What can be done that will make a difference next time?

The science for answering these questions is developing but is as yet far from definitive. Practitioners and researchers debate the wisdom of various approaches. Even acknowledged experts are uncertain about the effectiveness of different interventions. Is it better to target only at-risk students? Or should all students be alerted? Is it most effective to teach suicide prevention directly? Or should comprehensive health programs teach generic primary prevention skills such as communication, problem solving, and decision making?

As adolescent suicides have increased, families and communities have turned more and more to the schools for help. The schools have attempted to cope with the problem, but their efforts cannot end with the programs and policies implemented within their walls.

Youth suicide is a societal concern. In addition to providing educa-

---

4. With special thanks to Gary Nelson, Jacquelyn Sowers, Cynthia Lang, and Stu Cohen for their thoughtful review and critique of draft material.

tional programs, schools must consider as well how to coordinate with referral and treatment programs, how to communicate with family and friends and involve them constructively in school-based initiatives. Like the larger question of health education, suicide prevention may begin in the schools, but it must always be more than the school's responsibility.

This chapter is based on an extensive review of the literature, consultation with various experts, and the outcomes of focus groups with principals, teachers, and guidance counselors convened to further understand their concerns.[5] The chapter considers adolescent suicide in relation to other developmental and health issues faced by adolescents in America today. This chapter examines the supportive potential of the school environment. Major types of suicide prevention programs and evidence of their effectiveness are reviewed with recommendations to guide the educational programs.

Suicide Prevention Programs: General Considerations

Approaches to suicide prevention employed by schools over the last decade can generally be described as: (a) categorical or suicide-specific interventions that educate students about suicide; training programs for teachers, counselors, and sometimes parents to detect and refer adolescents at risk for suicide or mental illness to more in-depth services in the school or community; and (b) non-categorical or comprehensive, broad-based programs with a greater emphasis on primary prevention and skill building from K–12 in a school health education curriculum.

To date, the majority of suicide prevention programs have been categorical, instituted in reaction to recent suicides or attempted suicides in a school or community. Of 106 school-based suicide prevention programs surveyed, 104 dealt only with the topic of suicide and the other two were more generic (Smith, Eyman, Dyck, & Ryerson, 1987).[6] In 1986, these programs reached approximately 180,000 students (Shaffer, Garland, Gould, Fisher & Trautman, 1988). Historically, most programs

---

5. Participants in the focus group included: Vincent D'Antona and Thomas Trevisani, Arlington High School, Arlington, MA; Linda Wolfe, Charles Brown Junior High School, Newton, MA; Gail Stein and Linda Shapiro, Newton North High School, Newton, MA; and Norman Hyett, Newton South High School, Newton, MA. The focus group was held October 12, 1988 at Education Development Center in Newton, MA.

6. Personal communication with Kim Smith, Ph.D., The Menninger Clinic, Albuquerque, NM, September, 1988.

have offered secondary prevention, an attempt to prevent further harm to the same individual or involvement of additional students. It is estimated that less than 15 percent of the nation's schools offer primary prevention and school health education K–12, concerned with broad-based skill building.[7]

Primum Non Nocere

What can schools learn from the various approaches designed to protect youngsters to be sure that their efforts "Do No Harm?" Before reviewing the data on what works, it is important to point out that no suicide prevention program, categorical or comprehensive, has evaluated the impact of its intervention on actual suicide rates. The number of suicides in any one community is small. This fact, fortunate in personal terms, makes program assessment and detection of a statistically significant difference very difficult. The cost to implement and monitor an intervention intensive enough and of sufficient duration to capture evidence of change in actual rates would be prohibitive.

The sections that follow present the best evidence available to date in reviewing the effectiveness of various approaches to prevention: specific classroom instruction in suicide prevention; teacher training and referral; and primary prevention through comprehensive school health education in grades K–12.

Categorical Interventions

Classroom Instruction on Suicide Prevention

Suicide prevention education in the classroom usually includes a one-time, short program from an hour and a half to four hours in length (Shaffer, Bacon, Fisher, & Garland, 1987). Most of these programs teach students about the prevalence of suicide in their age group, typical warning signals, the availability of helping resources in the school and community, students' role in identifying and helping a suicidal adolescent, and behavioral skills adolescents can use to gain the trust and confidence of a potentially suicidal person.

There are few systematic evaluations of school-based suicide prevention programs. Those that do exist mostly provide information about

---

7. Personal communication with Clarence Pearson, National Center for Health Education, December 1988.

changes in student knowledge, attitudes, and perceptions of the program. Only a few give data on a program's ability to identify or screen young-sters in need of counseling, to make appropriate referrals to mental health agencies, and to reduce the number of suicide attempts. Although information about program impact on knowledge is important and necessary, it is insufficient. Since it is not feasible to measure effectiveness based on suicide rates, more research is needed to measure changes in students' self-efficacy, confidence and skill in seeking help, levels of anxiety and depression, detection and referral rates, and reduction in attempts.

Findings in program effectiveness in increasing student knowledge and attitudes are somewhat inconsistent. For example, students who completed a four-hour training course in a California school showed significant gains over a control group in understanding youth suicide prevention techniques (Nelson, 1987). Yet, students in New Jersey who participated in three similar suicide prevention programs showed little change in knowledge. Approximately 80 percent of the control students knew that suicide threats and attempts and the use and abuse of alcohol and drugs were warning signs of suicide risk, but the level of knowledge about these warning signs was no greater in the group exposed to the suicide prevention programs (Shaffer, Garland, & Whittle, 1987).

This study also found that students who had attempted suicide per-ceived the programs very differently from those who had not. Previous attempters were more likely to rate the programs unfavorably. They reported more often than non-attempters that the programs were disturb-ing or boring (Shaffer, Garland, & Whittle, 1987). Although the number of attempters was small, the evaluation still raises some questions about the effectiveness of these programs for those students at highest risk. The New Jersey study also found that between 5 percent and 20 percent of students in experimental and control groups expressed views that raise serious concern. Students stated that "under certain circumstances sui-cide was a reasonable solution to a problem and that they would not reveal the suicidal confidence of a friend or seek help from a mental health professional if they felt troubled" (Shaffer, Garland, & Whittle, 1987). The three-hour program had no effect on this view. Similarly, students in a California survey distributed to schools reported that the person they would most likely contact if they were contemplating suicide, and who would therefore be their most likely rescuer, would be a friend (Nelson, 1987).

The recent National Adolescent Student Health Survey (1988) confirms this view. Only 18 percent of the students said it would be "easy or very easy" to tell the school counselor, teacher, or a member of a friend's family if the friend was considering suicide. Only a third of the students said they "could locate a community agency for suicide prevention." Unfortunately, as Ross (1985) states, "Some of the very qualities that make peers the confidants of choice also make them dangerously inadequate as counselors and rescuers." Many students feel that to preserve the friendship, they must maintain the confidence of a friend.

If school programs are to teach youngsters about the risks of suicide and its typical warning signs, they must be very aggressive in trying to convince youngsters of the need to seek help for a friend, in teaching how to handle confidences and how to develop trust and encourage disclosure, and in supplying information on where to turn for help.

Few students in the New Jersey study understood either before or after the program that suicide was a feature of mental illness. Shaffer believes that since suicide does seem to be a feature of mental illness, programs must present it as such or they are likely to reinforce suicide as an adolescent's romantic response to stress or isolation from parents and other institutions (Shaffer, 1988).

The New Jersey evaluation, like a few others, looked beyond knowledge change to other indicators, such as identifying students wanting help or referrals, and those who had attempted suicide. The New Jersey program found that one value of the school-based program was that approximately 3 percent of the students identified themselves through the pre- and post-tests as being currently troubled or suicidal and wanting professional help. Similarly, in a suicide prevention program at a Dayton, Ohio, high school, experimental students who were pre- and post-tested and participated in a classroom presentation on suicide showed a statistically significant increase in willingness to confide in the teacher in contrast to a comparison group (Johnson, 1985). Ross (1980) found that there was an increase in numbers of referrals after suicide prevention programming was initiated in California. Whether this was due primarily to educating students, training teachers, or a symbiotic combination of the two was not specified or analyzed.

Emphasis on the help-seeking component is critical. Shaffer is concerned that classroom discussion of suicide makes it seem "normal" and discourages students from feeling uncomfortable enough to seek help. If schools or teachers choose to implement a program that involves some classroom discussion of suicide, they should make sure that the teaching includes clear up-to-date information on where to turn for help. One of the best strategies is to offer one-on-one follow-up counseling with trained personnel, preferably mental health professionals, to any pupil who admits to feeling more preoccupied with suicide after such a presentation.

Training Adults to Detect and Refer Students At Risk

Given the uncertainty of the utility of suicide education for students, some school districts have placed the responsibility for case identification and referral with adults: teachers, administrators, guidance counselors, and, on occasion, parents. The ongoing contact between adolescents and high school staff may provide an opportunity for early identification and effective management of suicidal behavior. By learning more about the warning signs associated with suicide and the community services available to adolescents, it is hoped that school personnel can make sure that those at risk are referred to treatment. School personnel have a wide variety of professional experiences and opportunities to interact with children and parents. Moreover, through the years they have gained an understanding of adolescent development, risk factors, and warning signs of adolescent depression and suicidality (Grob, Klein, & Eisen, 1983; Maag, Rutherford, & Parks, 1988). The viewpoints of teachers and other school personnel are based primarily on their actual observations of distressed adolescents, but their views appear to coincide with theoretical and empirical research on depression and suicidality. Teachers are often the first to notice these problems because the classroom provides a structural setting for assessing the student (Maag, Rutherford, & Parks, 1988). These findings indicate that it is within the scope of teachers and counselors to identify and refer adolescents who display symptoms of mental illness or suicide. With proper training, school faculty can play an important role in expediting referral to proper treatment for troubled adolescents.

It should be noted, however, that most lists of warning signs of suicide are brief and emphasize a recent onset of depression, i.e. changes in mood, decreasing sociability and a drop in school performance, increasing irritability, and some specific behaviors such as suicidal threats, drug and alcohol abuse, and giving away possessions (Shaffer, Bacon, Fisher, & Garland, 1987). They are not derived empirically from representative samples. Shaffer and others at the New York Psychiatric Institute are in the midst of a study to determine, by gathering information about deceased individuals, what these warning signs really are. Some preliminary findings indicate that a study sample of suicide completers had long-standing behavior and academic problems and were often users of drugs and alcohol. Only a small percentage displayed what has been viewed as the typical precursor or precipitator of suicide: an isolated major depressive disorder. These suicide completers were predominantly female (Shaffer & Gould, 1987).

Like the educational programs designed to teach students about suicide, evaluation of programs to train school faculty and staff in detection and referral has been confined predominantly to attitude and knowledge change. In one study, pre-tests and post-tests were administered to teachers who participated in an in-service suicide prevention program at a Dayton, Ohio high school. Teachers showed a significant increase in knowledge of resources from which to obtain aid for a suicidal young person and an increased knowledge of facts and myths concerning suicide (Johnson, 1985). In a review of youth suicide programs, Shaffer et al. (1987) surmised from comments and data they received from school staff that it would be helpful for staff to receive guidance on how to handle a referral to an outside agency. For this to be fully effective, however, schools must strengthen their formal ties with community agencies to form a support network when the school or a teacher anticipates or actually experiences a crisis.

Several programs have tried to include parents in an attempt to strengthen the link between home and school. These efforts might include meetings offered in conjunction with the PTA or during "parent night" functions. Often, these sessions are very similar to those given to school personnel (i.e. warning signs, myths and facts, referral resources), with the additional goal of improving communication between parent and child. However, attracting parents to such programs is difficult. A suicide prevention program in California found that parents were generally unwilling to participate (Nelson, 1987). This was particularly disturbing since "the young people who participated in the prevention program indicated that problems with parents appeared to them to be the major cause of youth suicide."

Parent education is a vital component. If parents can both recognize and understand the "problem" behaviors of their adolescents, they are more likely to act in appropriate rather than punitive ways. Workshops to educate parents about adolescent development might begin with a small, but interested group and expand over time. Rather than relying solely on workshops, however, other forms and channels of communication should be explored for this audience. Delivery systems that tap and link with the resources of the community should be explored, including cable television, religious groups, columns in local newspapers, and work-site education programs.

Comprehensive or Broad-Based Primary Prevention Programs

Because the examples from the professional literature reveal that concerns over contagion are to some extent warranted (Kreitman, Smith, & Tan, 1970; Shaffer, 1974; Phillips, 1984; Gould & Shaffer, 1986), many in the field have suggested alternative educational strategies for preventing suicide (Shaffer, Bacon, Fisher, & Garland, 1987).[8] Rather than teach the topic of suicide directly to students, they suggest that schools should provide a health education curriculum for all students that builds basic skills useful for managing a variety of health issues—in coping, problem solving, interpersonal communication and conflict resolution, and building self-esteem. This way, the course has some relevance to all students, and teachers can still detect and refer those at highest risk. A relatively small number of adolescents will attempt or commit suicide, but there are many with problems who can be helped by identification and by broader-based interventions and referral if other severe disorders are identified.

As noted health educator Dr. Robert Gould has explained so well, suicide, homicide, AIDS, and pregnancy are only the tip of the iceberg. We must address the developmental issues that underlie all the problems. We must support adolescents as they deal with identity formation, separation from parents, and greater attachments to peers. This is the time when all youngsters must develop the necessary coping strategies that can help them: communication skills, social skills, conflict resolution, and problem-solving skills. Educators must differentiate between programs that provide the vast majority of youngsters with coping skills to promote physical, emotional and social well-being, and programs that may prevent suicide among the few who may ultimately attempt it.

---

8. Also, personal communication with Kim Smith, Ph.D., The Menninger Clinic, Albuquerque, NM, September 1988 and with Jacquelyn Sowers, M.Ed., Sowers Associates, Hampton, NH, September 1988.

Building Problem-Solving Skills

"Primary prevention" is a term borrowed from the field of public health, and it usually includes efforts to reduce the factors that put the adolescent at risk for suicide and to enhance resistance to the environmental stressors that may make the young person vulnerable to suicide. Such instructional efforts can be targeted to all students between grades K–12 and are designed not just to reduce suicides but to alleviate or prevent many of the other problems of youth. The programs are complemented by counseling and other services in the school and community.

Unlike categorical suicide prevention programs, non-categorical programs usually are longer and ideally offer a planned scope and sequence for K–12 as an ongoing health curriculum. Health concerns are also integrated into overall school policy and practice; for example, no-smoking policies and healthy cafeteria foods support the curriculum. The primary prevention approach involves teaching students how to cope adequately with the stressors in their lives and creates a positive and supportive environment in the school.

It is believed that by teaching young people to manage stress and cope with adversity and depression, they can seek out solutions other than suicide. As Shaffer and Gould (1987, p. 20) state: "The stresses which precede a suicide are usually non-specific and we suspect that the mood which precedes a suicidal response is often a mixture of anger and with it a desire for revenge, as well as anxiety and an inability to think about other ways of coping with anger."

Thus, young people who possess the skills to see their way clear of crisis by choosing alternative solutions and overcoming obstacles will be able to avoid the negative mental health outcomes. Much of the support for this argument comes from the community psychology literature and the work of Spivack and Shure. Their work provides strong evidence that means-ends thinking, seeing viable alternatives, and identifying the consequences of actions are adaptive skills that teachers can learn and teach to their students. Problem solving, more than a curriculum, is a way of teaching and can be incorporated into any curriculum or any subject matter. Teachers can provide students with hypothetical problems and engage in dialogue with the class over solutions rather than giving students the answers.

This type of teaching can be used on real problems as well. One counselor in Ontario, Canada (Roberts, 1982) wrote about a student who displayed delinquent behavior during recess. This teacher decided that she would enlist the support of her fifth and sixth grade classroom in order to improve the student's behavior. The delinquent student and his parents agreed to the discussion sessions, and the class was asked to offer ideas as to why he acted the way he did and suggestions for better ways to handle daily events. The purpose of the discussion was to stimulate each child to help the other; the children helped each other solve problems and seek alternative solutions to their problems. Thus, they began to view themselves as a cohesive group. While this example is only a case study, it does offer some insight into alternative solutions for preventing delinquent behavior.

Spivack and Shure (1982, 1985) have identified the skills required to think through a problem which they have come to call Interpersonal Cognitive Problem Solving (ICPS). These skills include consequential thinking, causal thinking, and cognitive sensitivity to the possible interpersonal nature of the problem involving another person. The interpersonal problem-solving approach shows promise in the area of suicide prevention. Suicidal adolescents often lack the ability to see alternative solutions when faced with highly stressful situations.

While there has been no evaluation of the effectiveness of ICPS specifically on preventing suicides, a number of ICPS interventions have demonstrated significant behavioral impact, as summarized in Spivack and Shure (1982, 1985). Usually, ICPS interventions have been targeted at very young children in preschool or kindergarten; however, there have been successful interventions targeted at older populations. Some success in populations with special needs: hyperactive 7-year-olds (Camp & Bush, 1978, 1982); educable retarded 5- to 12-year-olds (Healey, 1977); emotionally disturbed fifth graders (Natov, 1981); learning disabled 8- to 12-year-olds (Weiner, 1978); young adult alcoholics (Intagliata, 1978); and short-term young adult inpatients (Coche & Flick, 1975). ICPS intervention has also helped to reduce the intensity of stressors experienced at transition to middle school (grade 6), including serious public and mental health problems from becoming involved with smoking or drinking to issues of coping with peer pressure, academic requirements, and the logistics of being in a large, unfamiliar school. The amount of stress experienced was also found to be directly related to the length of training (Elias, 1984).

Implementing Comprehensive School Health Education

What do we mean by the term "comprehensive school health education"? Broadly speaking, it is health education in a school setting that is planned and carried out with the purpose of maintaining, reinforcing, or enhancing the health, health-related skills, and health attitudes and practices of children and youth that are conducive to their good health.

Comprehensive school health programs traditionally encompass three interdependent components: health education (instruction), health services, and healthful school environment. The purposes of each of these program components complement and are complemented by the procedures and the activities of the others. Although such a program is school based, it is recognized that not just school personnel and students but their families and communities must be involved in its planning, implementation, and evaluation (National Professional School Health Education Organization, 1984).

The curricular component of comprehensive health education is based on the same principles of skill building described earlier, applied specifically to health and mental health decisions. The school health education evaluation demonstrated that school health education at the upper elementary level is an effective means of helping children improve their health knowledge and develop healthy attitudes (Cornell, 1985). This three-year study of four different health instructional programs (School Health Curriculum Project, now known as Growing Healthy; Health Education Curriculum Guide; Project Prevention; and High Blood Pressure) also found that all self-reported health skills and practices subscores were higher in health program classrooms, with the greatest differences recorded in decision-making skills. Significantly fewer students in the target programs began smoking in the seventh grade than in the comparison classrooms. While there is no clear link between these curricula and suicide prevention, the curricula have succeeded in improving skill building and in reducing other behaviors harmful to health.

The evaluation also found that the more time spent on the curriculum, the greater the learning. A minimum of 20–30 hours of instruction was necessary to produce changes in knowledge, attitudes, and behavior.

At the secondary level, Macro Systems, Inc., in Silver Spring, Maryland, under contract from the Centers for Disease Control, has recently completed an evaluation of the Teenage Health Teaching Modules (THTM), a comprehensive health education curriculum for grades 7 through 12

(1988). THTM differs from traditional health instruction, in that its materials are organized into developmental-based tasks of concern to adolescents rather than by content area. The nineteen modules include such titles as *Living with Feelings, Protecting Oneself and Others,* and *Communicating in Families.* Rather than imparting knowledge alone, the modules attempt to develop skills in self-assessment, communication, decision making, health advocacy, and healthy self-management.

The THTM evaluation included both outcome measures to determine whether or not the program worked, and process measures to determine how the program was implemented in classrooms and why it did or did not work. THTM's effectiveness was judged by curriculum-specific changes on each of three dimensions—knowledge, attitudes, and practices—and in terms of priority health behaviors (e.g. participation in appropriate physical activity; not smoking cigarettes). The THTM evaluation involved 149 schools and nearly 5,000 students in seven states. In each school, two classes took part in the study. A treatment class was pre-tested, taught THTM for a semester (approximately 40 classes), and post-tested. The control class was pre-tested and post-tested, without taking THTM or being exposed to other health content in the interim. Teachers kept detailed records on the activities they used in each THTM module, reported their attitudes toward the curriculum and how they used it, and provided information about their backgrounds and the setting in which THTM was used.

Results indicate that the THTM curriculum was effective in improving students' health-related knowledge, attitudes, and, to a lesser extent, the practices and behaviors of secondary school students. For example, THTM had a statistically significant effect on two measures: the percentage of students not smoking during a 30-day period and the mean incidence of drug use during a 30-day period.

Teacher training had a statistically significant effect on teachers' self-reports of feeling prepared to teach the material. It also had a positive effect on their fidelity to using the activities as presented in the teacher's guide and, most importantly, on student learning.

The challenges are great in health education evaluations, because many of the changes occur outside the classroom and in later years. It is also difficult to distinguish which aspects (e.g. the curriculum, the school environment, the home environment) have a greater role to play in the health behavior change.

Nevertheless, the positive effects of comprehensive school health education in teaching skills that encourage youngsters to adopt healthy behaviors show that such instruction offers promise as one important component of an educational strategy for preventing youth suicide.

Summary and Recommendations

The young people in our schools are society's most valuable—and valued—resource. When a young person dies by his or her own hand, more than the life, and future life, of that person is lost. So, too, is a measure of hope.

Educators, administrators, and counselors working in schools all have a responsibility to take action, not only on behalf of the individuals who are at risk, but also in aid and support of those around them. For every individual who needs direct and immediate help, there are many more who need assistance in knowing what they can do that will make a difference.

Although there still are unanswered questions (and pitfalls to avoid), there is still a knowledge base to guide action. Working in our communities, with care, carefulness, and compassion, school personnel can move forward to learn more about preventing the tragic and early death of young people and to incorporate in their schools the policies, programs, and practices that offer the best hope of preventing this loss.

The field has learned a great deal from the suicide-specific classroom programs. Some students through a pre-test questionnaire may identify themselves as being in need of help, but friends may not divulge their knowledge of a friend who is depressed or suicidal to teachers or parents. The programs may increase the referral of students to mental health services, but many students still do not know where or how to seek appropriate help or services for themselves or a friend. Students most at risk may be bored or alienated by suicide-specific instruction. Finally, students do not associate suicide with mental illness. Clearly, discrete suicide education programs of three to four hours are insufficient for young people at highest risk of suicide and also cannot meet the needs of an increasing number of students who are adopting health-compromising behaviors. These findings suggest that schools proceed with caution. The challenge is to build on this knowledge base so that future efforts not only "do no harm" but remove harm.

In conclusion, what can school personnel learn from past efforts to build programs of tomorrow? The causes of suicide—biological, psychological, and sociocultural—are complex and interrelated. An effective response, given the range of mental and emotional health needs of young people today, is the joining together of schools, families, and communities in a comprehensive approach.

References

Camp, B. W., & Bush, M. A. (1978). *The classroom "think aloud" program.* Paper presented at the meeting of the American Psychological Association, Toronto.

Camp, B. W., & Bush, M. A. (1981). *Think aloud: Increasing social and cognitive skills: A problem-solving program for children, primary level.* Champaign, IL: Research Press.

Coche, A., & Flick, A. (1975). Problem-solving skills of an alcoholic population. *Journal of Consulting and Clinical Psychology, 91,* 19–29.

Elias, M. J. (1980). *Developing instrumental strategies for television-based preventive mental health curricula in elementary school setting.* Unpublished doctoral dissertation, University of Connecticut, Storrs.

Elias, M. J. (1984). *Project aware: Social problem-solving as prevention model.* (Progress report, No. 36828). Washington, D.C.: National Institute of Mental Health.

Gould, M. S., & Shaffer, D. (1986). The impact of suicide in television movies: Evidence of imitation. *New England Journal of Medicine, 315,* 690–694.

Grob, M. C., Klein, A. A., & Eisen, S. V. (1983). The role of the high school professional in identifying and managing adolescent suicidal behavior. *Journal of Youth and Adolescence, 12,* 163–173.

Healey, K. (1977). *An investigation of the relationship between certain social cognitive abilities and social behavior, and the efficacy of training in social cognitive skills for elementary retarded-educable children.* Unpublished doctoral dissertation, Bryn Mawr College, Bryn Mawr, Pa.

Intagliata, J. (1978). Increasing the interpersonal problem-solving skills of an alcoholic population. *Journal of Consulting and Clinical Psychology, 46,* 489–498.

Johnson, W. Y. (1985). Classroom discussion of suicide: An intervention tool for the teacher. *Contemporary Education, 56,* 114–117.

Kreitman, N., Smith, P., & Tan, E. S. (1986). The impact of suicide in television movies: Evidence of imitation. *New England Journal of Medicine, 315,* 690–694.

Maag, J. W., Rutherford, R. B. Jr., & Parks, B. T. (1988). Secondary school professionals' ability to identify depression in adolescents. *Adolescence, 23,* 73–82.

National Adolescent Student Health Survey. (1988). American School Health Association, Association for the Advancement of Health Education, Society for Public Health Education. "Injury Prevention Fact Sheet."

National Professional School Health Education Organization. (1984). Comprehensive school health education: a definition. *Journal of School Health, 54,* 312–315.

Natov, I. (1981). *An intervention to facilitate interpersonal cognitive problem-solving skills and behavioral adjustment among emotionally handicapped children.* Unpublished doctoral dissertation, Fordham University, New York.

Nelson, F. L. (1987). Evaluation of a youth suicide prevention school program. *Adolescence, 23,* 813–825.

Phillips, D. (1984). Teenage and adult temporal fluctuations in suicide and auto fatalities. In H. S. Sudak, A. B. Ford, & N. B. Rushforth (Eds.), *Suicide in the young.* Boston, MA: John Wright PSG, Inc.

Pine, P. (1985). *Critical issues report, promoting health education in schools: Problems and solutions.* American Association of School Administrators.

Roberts, J. (1982). Peer facilitating: A prevention program for delinquent behavior. *School Guidance Worker, 38,* 45–47.

Ross, C. P. (1980). Mobilizing schools for suicide prevention. *Suicide and Life Threatening Behavior, 10,* 239–243.

Ross, C. P. (1985). Teaching children the facts of life and death: suicide prevention in the schools. In M. L. Peck, N. L. Farberow, & R. E. Litman (Eds.), *Youth suicide.* New York: Springer Publishing Company, Inc.

Shaffer, D. (1974). Suicide in childhood and early adolescence. *Journal of Child Psychology and Psychiatry, 15,* 275–291.

Shaffer, D., Bacon, K., Fisher, P., & Garland, A. (1987). *Review of youth suicide prevention programs.* Report prepared for the Governor of New York State's Task Force on Youth Suicide Prevention.

Shaffer, D., Garland, A., & Whittle, B. (1987). *An evaluation of three youth suicide prevention programs in New Jersey.* Report prepared for the New Jersey State Department of Health and Human Services.

Shaffer, D., & Gould, M. (1987). Study of completed and attempted suicide in adolescents. Progress Report: National Institute of Mental Health.

Shaffer, D., Garland, A., Gould, M., Fisher, P., & Trautman, P. (1988). Preventing teenage suicide: A critical review. *Journal of the American Academy of Child and Adolescent Psychiatry, 27,* 675–687.

Smith, K., Eyman, J., Dyck, R., & Ryerson, D. (1987). Report of a survey of school-based programs. Unpublished.

Spivack, G., & Shure, M. (1982). Interpersonal cognitive problem solving and clinical theory. In B. Lahey & A. E. Kazdin (Eds.), *Advances in child clinical psychology, Volume 5.* New York: Plenum Press.

Spivack, G., & Shure, M. (1985). ICPS and beyond: Centripetal and centrifugal forces. *American Journal of Community Psychology, 13,* 226–243.

Weiner, J. A. (1978). *A theoretical model of the affective and social development of hearing disabled children.* Unpublished doctoral dissertation, University of Michigan.

Chapter 7

THE WERTHER EFFECT
AND YOUTH SUICIDE CLUSTERS

David A. Jobes and Peter Cimbolic

Introduction

Professional and public attention focused on the possible stimulus effect of another's suicide on imitative behavior can be traced back over two hundred years to the 1774 Goethe novel, *The Sorrows of Young Werther*. The notion that examples of suicidal behavior may influence subsequent imitative behavior has come to be known as the "Werther effect" (Phillips, 1974). In recent years, attention has become increasingly focused on suicide "contagion" and the outbreak of suicide "clusters" among the young.

History of the Werther Effect

Goethe's controversial novel, which allegedly led to a rash of youthful copycat suicides, was widely read throughout Europe. The novel about a young martyr of unrequited love (who ultimately commits suicide) created a new international style of romantic suffering (Alvarez, 1976). According to Friedenthal (1965), there was a virtual Werther epidemic for decades in Germany, England, France, Holland, and Scandinavia. Some young men imitated their fictional hero by dressing in blue tailcoats and yellow waistcoats (caricatures of Werther), while more serious imitators killed themselves by reenacting Werther's suicide by gunshot to the head.

Although the reported widespread imitation of Werther's suicide was never empirically validated, authorities were apparently concerned enough to ban the book in several areas including Italy, Leipzig, and Copenhagen (Phillips, 1974). Since Goethe's era, suicides described in fiction have been thought to stimulate subsequent imitative suicidal behavior. Indeed, as discussed by Motto (1967), one author claimed in 1845 that no fact is "better established in science" than the imitative effect of suicide (Brigham, 1845).

Alvarez (1976) provides an excellent historical review of suicide in the literature of the nineteenth and twentieth centuries. Prior to the end of the eighteenth century, suicide had largely not been evident in art or literature. However, the Romantics of the late eighteenth century elevated suicide as a major theme, if not a preoccupation. While it is impossible to measure the actual impact of suicide portrayed in literature and art had on the actual incidence of suicide, it has long been believed that suicide portrayed in literature and art has perhaps contributed to imitative suicide deaths.

The role that journalistic reporting of suicides in the press plays in subsequent suicides has been hotly debated for over 100 years. Motto (1967) traces the controversy back to 1894 when the *New York Times* charged that an article about the relationship between sin and suicide published in the *New York World* precipitated a rash of suicides. Motto (1967) notes that this controversy peaked in the first decade of the 1900s. During this period, both Phelps (1911) and Wadsworth (1911) linked newspaper accounts of suicide to subsequent suicidal and criminal acts. The American Academy of Medicine in 1911 devoted a section of its annual meeting exclusively to imitative effect of news stories. In the same year, the National Association of Retail Druggists protested explicit accounts of overdose deaths in the public press (Hemenway, 1911). Motto (1967) described concerns about newspaper stories' effects on suicidal behavior. This was not limited to the United States, as both American and British health officials fought to prohibit journalists from explicitly reporting accounts of suicides.

Suicide modeling effects are not a new phenomenon or necessarily unique to the United States. Berman (1986) noted that Freud and his colleagues discussed their concerns about suicide suggestibility, imitation, and clusters (among other topics related to suicide) at a 1910 meeting of the Vienna Psychoanalytic Society. Recent concerns about self-destructive modeling effect of heavy-metal music were preceded by similar fears over fifty years ago on another continent. Robbins and Conroy (1983) report that eighteen youth suicides in 1936 were linked to a popular love song entitled "Gloomy Sunday" in Budapest, Hungary.

What has changed in the past 100 years has been the movement from anecdotal-based speculations about the effects of modeling on suicidal behavior to data-based investigations. While important research and methodological progress has increased our knowledge about imitative effects, the data-based literature still remains somewhat contradictory.

Research and the Werther Effect

According to Lester (1972) and Phillips (1974), results from initial attempts to study suggestion or imitation were largely inconclusive. Unfortunately, many studies which have suggested imitative effects could also be explained by other factors. Motto (1967) studied suicide rates in seven cities during newspaper strikes (expecting to find decreases in suicide rates in the absence of newspaper modeling effects) but found no significant decreases in suicide during the strikes and therefore no newspaper modeling effect. In a report of double suicides among psychiatric hospital patients, Crawford and Willis (1966) examined six pairs of suicides for imitative effects and found evidence of imitation in three of the pairs with no apparent imitative effect in the remaining three pairs. Seiden (1968) studied five suicides in a one-month period in Berkeley and found no evidence of imitation. Weiss (1958) observed that survivors of a spouse's suicide may attempt suicide on the anniversary of their loved-one's death. Such behavior might reflect imitation but may also be an acute anniversary grief reaction. Kreitman et al. (1969) observed that suicide attempters have a large number of suicidal friends. While this may reflect imitation, it may reflect that suicide-prone people seek out each other. Results of these early studies led Lester to conclude in 1972 that contagion and suggestibility were difficult to confirm or rule out.

David Phillips's (1974) sociologically oriented line of research has generated a great deal of interest, research, and debate. Employing a quasi-experimental method on monthly aggregate suicide data, Phillips (1974) examined the influence of suicide stories on the front page of the *New York Times* between 1947 and 1968 on subsequent suicide rates and found that suicide rates did increase immediately after the publication of suicide stories. These results indicated that suicides increased proportionally to the amount of publicity devoted to a story about suicide. These suicide increases were found to be restricted mainly to the area in which the story was publicized. Since this initial study, Phillips (1979, 1980a, 1980b, 1982, 1983) has extended his investigations to include homicides, single-car motor vehicle fatalities, and airplane accidents. Phillips (1977, 1979) conducted additional studies which indicate that some imitative suicides may be disguised as accidents. Bollen and Phillips

(1982) and Phillips and Carstensen (1986) replicated these imitative effects and extended them to televised news suicide stories.

Some researchers have criticized Phillips's methodology and in re-analyses could not support some of his findings (Kessler & Stripp, 1984; Baron & Reiss, 1985). Wasserman (1984) using a different methodology reexamined and extended Phillips's original data set from 1974 to 1977. Using a multivariate time-series analysis, Wasserman (1984) controlled for economic shifts, seasonal effects, average duration of unemployment, and war. Results revealed no significant linkage between the national suicide rate and stories of "prominent" suicides on the front page of the *New York Times.* However, examining the influence of only celebrity (as operationally differentiated from "prominent") suicides revealed a significant rise in national suicides in the month following a celebrity suicide. Wasserman therefore argues the suicidal imitation effect identified by Phillips is operational but more selective than originally hypothesized.

Phillips and Carstensen (1986) attempted to examine imitative effects specifically among youthful populations. Results indicated that national rates of teenage suicide rose significantly just after news or feature stories about suicide were broadcasted on television. This was specific to teenagers and not adults (ages 20 and above), and more so for females. The authors suggest these results support the belief that teenagers, particularly females, may be more susceptible to fads, fashions, and imitation.

A related line of research examined the potential effects of suicide depicted in television movies on subsequent youthful imitative behavior. Gould and Shaffer (1986) studied variations in the numbers of suicides and attempts by teenagers in the greater New York area two weeks before and after television broadcasts of four fictional films about suicide. They found that the mean number of attempts in the two-week periods after the broadcasts was significantly greater than the mean number of attempts before the broadcast. Moreover, there was a significant increase in completed suicides (than would be predicted) following three of four broadcasts.

Attempts to replicate these data have produced mixed results. Phillips and Paight (1987) using the same methodology did not find increases in teenage suicide in either California or Pennsylvania after broadcasts of the same four films. Using a nationwide sample of suicide cases, Berman (1988) did not find increased suicides following three of the films, although imitation of method was linked to one of the films.

There is a clear need for further refinement of research methods and replication of previous studies. Berman (1988) asserts that additional research is needed which focuses more sharply on specific aspects of the interaction between fictional stimuli and individuals predisposed to imitation. Replication of these studies is needed, as there are significant potential implications for the media which must find a balance between freedom of speech and responsible journalism.

Summary of Werther Effect

While many studies have confirmed imitative effects, other investigations have provided inconclusive or contradictory results. Despite the mixed empirical results, the prevailing opinion appears to be that imitative effects do exist. However, as Berman (1988) has noted, the potential effects of imitative behavior depend on a complex interaction among characteristics of the stimulus, the observer of that stimulus, and conditions of time and geography. The exact influence of environmental variables is still uncertain, but as research continues and methodology improves (on both macro and micro levels) the mysteries of the Werther effect may be revealed.

The Suicide Clustering Phenomena

A related but somewhat different focus of imitative suicidal behavior has centered on reported "clusters" of youth suicides. The occurrence of suicide clusters is perhaps one of the most disturbing phenomena of youth suicide. Berman (1986) has defined a suicide cluster as a higher than expected frequency of suicidal behaviors within a certain geographic area over a given period of time, suggesting some connection between these behaviors. Gould, Wallenstein, and Davidson (1989) point out suicide epidemics have been reported from ancient times to today (e.g. Bakwin, 1957; Popow, 1911). Recently, a number of suicide outbreaks have been reported. Eisele, Frisino, Haglund, and Reay (1985), Curran (1987), Coleman (1987), and Davidson and Gould (1988) describe highly publicized recent clusters of youth suicide behavior in various parts of the United States—King County (Seattle), Washington; Westchester County, New York; Clear Lake and Plano, Texas; Leominster, Massachusetts; and Bergenfield, New Jersey.

For example, Robbins and Conroy (1983) have described a series of suicidal behaviors and subsequent attempts which occurred in Chappaqua, New York. In 1978 this small suburban community experienced two adolescent suicide deaths within a six-month period which were subsequently followed by five hospital admissions for suicide attempts and an admission for suicidal ideation within seven weeks of the second suicide. The six suicidal patients were found to be part of a group of students from the same high school who had visited each other during each others' hospitalizations for suicidal behaviors. The clear implication in this and other clusters is that youthful peers seem to influence or serve as models for suicidal behaviors, triggering subsequent suicidal imitation.

Research on Suicide Clusters

Empirical research in suicide clustering and contagion has been limited until recently. In their critical review of the topic, Gould, Wallenstein, and Davidson (1989) discussed some of the ongoing empirical studies which are attempting to investigate possible suicide clusters while employing stricter research models. These authors found that cluster studies basically employ two different research strategies: (a) the use of psychological autopsies; and (b) the use of epidemiological/statistical "time-space" analyses.

PSYCHOLOGICAL AUTOPSY STUDIES. The psychological autopsy is an investigatory procedure which attempts to reconstruct the psychological life-style of the decedent, their pre-morbid behaviors, and the psychosocial events which preceded the death (see Brent, 1989). This technique is used in suicide cluster research to identify possible mechanisms of contagion (such as whether cluster decedents directly know each other, have indirect knowledge of a community suicide through the news media, or are members of the same social network).

As discussed by Gould, Wallenstein, and Davidson (1989), preliminary analyses have provided some information which may clarify the etiology of clusters. It appears that decedents may not have direct contact with each other but may have indirect knowledge of local suicides through the news media. Some clusters may have a combination of members from one social network and individuals who did not know each other directly. Degree of acquaintance for those who know the decedent appears to vary widely. It also appears that similar methods of attempt may occur within a cluster, suggesting imitative effects. It is important to note that results of the initial psychological autopsy studies are still preliminary and further study is needed to more fully understand how contagion effects work.

TIME-SPACE STUDIES. A different approach to cluster studies employs the use of statistical and epidemiological models to assess temporal and geographic elements of suicide clusters. Phillips and Carstensen (1986) note, from a purely statistical/empirical perspective, that most efforts to document clusters of suicide have been anecdotal and alternative explanations for clusters are not always assessed. It is very difficult to interpret sporadic reports of suicide "outbreaks," in that some "clusters" appear by random chance alone. From an empirical perspective, it is crucial to determine whether "outbreaks" occur to an extent greater than would be predicted by random chance variation. Such "time-space" statistical research of clusters could provide support for the imitative effects of suicide. However, as Gould, Wallenstein, and Davidson (1989) point out, surveillance and systematic (replicable) research is difficult to undertake, since there are not yet standard operational definitions of suicide cluster time and space parameters.

Initial studies are underway, but thus far none have empirically confirmed that clustering is a phenomena that exists beyond random fluctuation (see discussions by Phillips & Carstensen, 1986; Berman, 1986; Rosenberg, Smith, Davidson, & Conn, 1987). Gould, Wallenstein, and Davidson (1989) in their review of this research describe the various time-space methods (and their limitations) which are currently being used to determine if suicide clusters are (statistically) "real," if clusters occur primarily among youth, and if the proportion of clusters tend to change over time.

As one example of this epidemiological approach to studying clusters, Clark (1989) recently reported preliminary findings of his research team. They developed a cluster distribution test which provides a statistical model using Poisson distributions as a tool to determine if the observed number of suicides is greater than the expected number of suicides for a given time, location, and population. An initial application of this method in Cook County, Illinois, between 1977 and 1987 did *not* demonstrate any statistically significant evidence of youthful suicide clusters for this time period (Clark, 1989).

While epidemiological time-space research thus far has not statistically revealed suicide clusters as an empirical reality, the development of operational definitions, continued monitoring and surveillance, and additional studies using similar and new methodology will provide important information to help understand how suicide clusters occur.

Concerns and Response

While researchers continue to study and debate the cluster phenomena, the occurrence of apparently related youth suicide behavior is very real and terrifying to those communities which have been exposed it. O'Carroll, Mercy, and Steward (1988) point out that while the contagion hypothesis has not yet been empirically validated, the sheer preponderance of anecdotal evidence suggests that suicides which occur later in a cluster often appear to have been influenced in many ways by earlier suicides in the same cluster.

The Centers for Disease Control (CDC) has worked closely with various state and local health agencies to investigate and respond to apparent clusters of suicides and attempts. O'Carroll, Mercy, and Steward (1988) describe that an atmosphere of crisis and intense concern among parents, students, school officials, and others occurs within the community experiencing a suicide cluster. Community leaders are then faced with the challenge of preventing the further expansion of the cluster while managing an intense community crisis.

In direct response to the needs of a community to manage the various aspects of a suicide cluster, the CDC has published a set of ten recommendations for preventing and containing suicide clusters (O'Carroll, Mercy, and Steward, 1988). Complete copies of these recommendations are available through the CDC.

Summary of Suicide Clusters

The occurrence of suicide clusters in small geographic areas over a discrete period of time has only recently become a focus for empirical research. While studies are underway, a real need has emerged for coordinated community responses to contain clusters while simultaneously addressing the individual crises. Significant steps have been initiated to assist community leaders, but additional research and focus is needed to more fully understand and prevent the terrifying and tragic clustering of youthful suicides.

References

Alvarez, A. (1976). Literature in nineteenth and twentieth centuries. In S. Perlin (Ed.), *A handbook for the study of suicide.* New York: Oxford University Press.

Bakwin, H. (1957). Suicide in children and adolescents. *Journal of Pediatrics, 50,* 749–769.

Baron, J. N., & Reiss, P. C. (1985). Same time, next year: Aggregate analyses of the mass media and violent behavior. *American Sociological Review, 50,* 347–363.

Berman, A. L. (1986). Adolescent suicide: Issues and challenges. In R. B. Shearin (Ed.), *Seminars in adolescent medicine.* New York: Thieme Medical Publishers.

Berman, A. L. (1986). A critical look at our adolescence: Notes on turning 18 (and 75). *Suicide and Life-Threatening Behavior, 16,* 1–12.

Berman, A. L. (1988). Fictional depiction of suicide in television films and imitation effects. *American Journal of Psychiatry, 145,* 982–986.

Bollen, K. A., & Phillips, D. P. (1982). Imitative suicides: A national study of the effects of television news stories. *American Sociological Review, 47,* 802–809.

Brent, D. A. (1989). The psychological autopsy: Methodological considerations for the study of adolescent suicide. *Suicide and Life-Threatening Behavior, 19,* 43–57.

Brigham, A. (1844). Statistics of suicides in the United States. *American Journal of Insanity, 1,* 225–234.

Clark, D. C. (1989). A method for evaluating suicide clusters. Paper presented at the 22nd annual meeting of the American Association of Suicidology, San Diego, California.

Crawford, J. P., & Willis, J. H. (1966). Double suicide in psychiatric hospital patients. *British Journal of Psychiatry,* 1231–1235.

Curran, D. K. (1987). *Adolescent suicidal behavior.* Washington: Hemisphere Publishing Corporation.

Davidson, L., & Gould, M. S. (1988). Contagion as a risk factor for youth suicide. In USDHHS: Report of the Secretary's Task Force on Youth Suicide. Volume 2: Risk factors for youth suicide. Washington, DC: U.S. Government Printing Office.

Eisele, J. W., Frisino, J., Haglund, W. D., & Reay, D. T. (1985). Teenage suicide in King County, Washington. Proceedings of the Eighteenth Annual Meeting of the American Association of Suicidology (Toronto, Canada).

Friedenthal, R. (1965). *Goethe: His life and times.* New York: World Publishing Company.

Gould, M. S., & Shaffer, D. (1986). The impact of suicide in television movies: Evidence of imitation. *New England Journal of Medicine, 315,* 690–694.

Gould, M. S., Wallenstein, S., & Davidson, L. (1989). Suicide clusters: A critical review. *Suicide and Life-Threatening Behavior, 19,* 17–29.

Hemenway, H. (1911). To what extent are suicide and crimes against the person due to suggestion from the press? *Bulletin of the American Academy of Medicine, 12,* 307–315.

Kessler, R. C., & Stipp, H. (1984). The impact of fictional television stories on U.S. fatalities: A replication. *American Journal of Sociology, 90,* 151–167.

Kreitman, N., Smith, P., & Tan, E. (1969). Attempted suicide in social networks. *British Journal of Preventive Social Medicine, 23,* 116–123.

Lester, D. (1972). *Why people kill themselves.* Springfield, IL: Charles C Thomas.

Motto, J. A. (1967). Suicide and suggestibility—The role of the press. *American Journal of Psychiatry, 124,* 252–256.

O'Carroll, P. W., Mercy, J. A., & Steward, J. A. (1988). CDC recommendations for a community plan for the prevention and containment of suicide clusters. *Morbidity and Mortality Weekly Report, 37,* 1–12.

Phelps, E. (1911). Neurotic books and newspapers as factors in the mortality of suicide and crime. *Bulletin of American Academy of Medicine, 12,* 264–306.

Phillips, D. P. (1974). The influence of suggestion on suicide: Substantive and theoretical implications of the werther effect. *American Sociological Review, 39,* 340–354.

Phillips, D. P. (1977). Motor vehicle fatalities increase just after publicized suicide stories. *Science, 196,* 1464–1465.

Phillips, D. P. (1979). Suicide, motor vehicle fatalities and the mass media: Evidence toward a theory of suggestion. *American Journal of Sociology, 84,* 1150–1174.

Phillips, D. P. (1980a). Airplane accidents, murder and the mass media: Toward a theory of imitation and suggestion. *Social Forces, 58,* 1001–1024.

Phillips, D. P. (1980b). The deterrent effect of capital punishment: New evidence of an old controversy. *American Journal of Sociology, 86,* 139–148.

Phillips, D. P. (1982). The impact of fictional television stories on U.S. adult fatalities: New evidence on the effect of the mass media on violence. *American Journal of Sociology, 87,* 1340–1359.

Phillips, D. P. (1983). The impact of mass media violence on U.S. homicides. *American Sociological Review, 48,* 560–568.

Phillips, D. P., & Carstensen, L. L. (1986). Clustering of teenage suicides after television news stoirs about suicide. *New England Journal of Medicine, 315,* 685–689.

Phillips, D. P., & Paight, D. J. (1987). The impact of televised movies about suicide: A replicative study. *New England Journal of Medicine, 317,* 809–811.

Popow, N. M. (1911). The present epidemic of school suicides in Russia. *Nevrol Nestnik (Kazan), 18,* 312–355, 592–646.

Range, L. M. (1987). Suicide contagion among adolescents: Family repercussions. Suicide in the Family. *Symposium at the 95th Annual Convention of the American Psychological Association,* New York, New York.

Robbins, D., & Conroy, R. (1983). A cluster of adolescent suicide attempts: Is suicide contagious? *Journal of Adolescent Health Care, 3,* 253–255.

Rosenberg, M. L., Smith, J. C., Davidson, L. E., & Conn, J. M. (1987). The emergence of youth suicide: An epidemiologic analysis and public health perspective. *American Review of Public Health, 8,* 417–440.

Seiden, R. H. (1968). Suicide behavior contagion on a college campus. In N. Farberow (Ed.), *Proceedings of the Fourth International Conference on Suicide Prevention,* 360–367.

Wadsworth, W. (1911). The newspapers and crime. *Bulletin of the American Academy of Medicine, 12,* 316–325.

Wasserman, I. M. (1984). Imitation and suicide: A reexamination of the werther effect. *American Sociological Review, 49,* 427–436.

NAME INDEX

SUBJECT INDEX